OFF SCREEN

OFF SCREEN

Women and film in Italy

Edited by Giuliana Bruno
and Maria Nadotti

Foreword by
LAURA MULVEY

R

ROUTLEDGE

LONDON AND NEW YORK

First published in 1988 by Routledge
11 New Fetter Lane, London EC4P 4EE

Published in the USA by Routledge
in association with Routledge, Chapman and Hall Inc.
29 West 35th Street, New York, NY 10001

The collection as a whole © 1988 Routledge; the individual contributions
© 1988 the contributors and translators

Typeset by Boldface Typesetters, London EC1
Printed in Great Britain at
The University Press, Cambridge.

British Library Cataloguing in Publication Data

Off screen: women and film in Italy.
   1. Moving-pictures – Italy   2. Women in moving-pictures
   I. Bruno, Giuliana   II. Nadotti, Maria
   791.43'09'09352042   PN1995.9.W6
   ISBN 0–415–00856–5
   ISBN 0–415–00857–3   Pbk

Library of Congress Cataloging-in-Publication Data

Off screen: women and film in Italy/edited by Giuliana Bruno and Maria
   Nadotti: foreword by Laura Mulvey.
      p. cm.
   Some papers translated from Italian.
   Papers presented at a seminar on 'Italian and American directions:
   women's film theory and practice,' held in New York, Dec. 1984.
   Filmography: p.
   Bibliography: p.
   Includes index
      ISBN 0–415–00856–5   ISBN 0–415–00857–3 (pbk.)
      1. Feminism and motion pictures – Congresses.   2. Women in
   motion pictures – Italy – Congresses.   I. Bruno, Giuliana.   II.
   Nadotti, Maria.
   PN1995.9.W6035   1988
   791.43'01'50945 – dc19   87–30778
                                    CIP

Contents

PART II   CRITICISM: THEORY/PRACTICE

PART III   FILM PRODUCTION

Notes on contributors

Lucilla Albano (Portogruaro, 1947) teaches history of cinema in the Italian department at the University of Florence. Mainly interested in theory, her research focuses on the relationship between psychoanalysis and cinema. Her essays have been published in magazines including *Nuovi Argomenti* and *Filmcritica*. She is editor of *Il divano di Freud*, a book of memoires of Freud's patients.

Giulia Alberti (Firenze, 1946) is a film critic and theorist whose writing focuses on women and film. Film analysis is one of the subjects she has taught at the Albedo Film School in Milan. As an artist, she works with stained glass.

Giovanna Grignaffini (Bologna, 1949) teaches history of cinema at the University of Bologna and is an editor of the film quarterly *Cinema e Cinema*. She has widely published on film as well as television (including pieces on René Clair, the French *nouvelle vague*, Weimar cinema) and co-edited with Piera Detassis a book on women and film entitled *Sequenza segreta*.

Lea Melandri (Fusignano, 1941) is a feminist theorist. A collection of her writings has been published with the title *L'infamia originaria*. Her latest writings on psychoanalysis are to be collected in *L'estasi e il gelo*. Ms Melandri taught at the adult education school of Affori from 1974 to 1986 and wrote a 'Ms Lonelyhearts' column in a teenage girls' magazine from 1984 to 1986. She is currently Chief-Editor of the feminist quarterly, *Lapis*.

Paola Melchiori (Treviso, 1948) is co-ordinator of the single-subject courses and adult education courses organized by the trade unions in Milan. Mainly interested in theory, she has worked and written on women and culture, and her articles have been published in magazines including the feminist quarterly *DWF*. She is co-author with Anna Scattigno of the book *Simone Weil*, and editor of *Verifica d'identita*, a collection of feminist writings.

Annabella Miscuglio (Lecce, 1939) has been making experimental films, documentaries, and videos since 1971. She co-directed the famous *Processo per stupro* (1978), *A.A.A. Offresi* (1979, a controversial documentary on prostitution), and the video *I fantasmi del fallo* (1980). In 1967, she co-founded the Filmstudio '70 in Rome, a show-case for independent and avant-garde films.

Adriana Monti (Milano, 1951) is a film and video-maker. She directed the Albedo Film School in Milan in 1983 and 1984 and has worked for RAI, the Italian national television company. Her recent works include a documentary on women textile workers *Filo a catena* (1986), and she is working on a feature film, *Gentile Signora*.

Patrizia Violi (Bologna, 1949) teaches semiotics at the University of Bologna and is an editor of the semiotic studies quarterly *Vs*. Her publications include, in 1977, a book-length analysis of the language of left-wing newspapers, and, in 1980, a book on the analysis of discourse. She has recently published a book on sexual difference in language and language theory, entitled *L'infinito singolare*.

Acknowledgements

This book owes a great deal to Laura Mulvey and Rosamund Howe. At a very critical moment, Laura came forward to support it, and, together with Rosamund, offered to work on the manuscript, to make our 'alien' writings speak to an Anglo-American readership. Our thanks to Rosamund and Laura for a gesture which is very meaningful to us and has made it possible to publish this book. Acknowledging our personal gratitude for their support, we also appreciate that their help has enabled the circulation of Italian feminist work.

We would like to thank E. Ann Kaplan for first introducing the idea of the book to the publisher. We are grateful to Teresa de Lauretis, Andrew Fierberg, Annette Michelson, and Janet Staiger for their support and suggestions along the way.

The book itself is also a way to thank all the women who participated in the Conference 'Italian and American Directions: Women's Film Theory and Practice' and contributed in making it possible and successful. Our acknowledgement for their generous help in different aspects of the organization of the event, among many, goes to Iris Cahn, Shirley Clarke, Joan Copjec, Fausta Daldini, Joie Lee, Elettra Nerbosi, Yvonne Rainer, Antonella Russo, Susan Seidelman, Amy Taubin, and Debbie Zimmerman.

Foreword

LAURA MULVEY

The seminar 'Italian and American directions: women's film theory and practice' took place in New York in December 1984. It was a moment of great pleasure and excitement. For me, part of the pleasure, on an immediate level, lay in the almost dream-like experience of seeing friends whom I associate with two quite distant places, meet and get to know each other with a warmth and energy that was reminiscent of the early days of the Women's Movement. And for me, as a Canadian national resident in Britain (thus both North American and European), there was a particular pleasure in being able to identify with the groups from each side of the Atlantic while being extraneous to both. The excitement, on an immediate level, lay in the success of the seminar's project of bringing the two feminist cultures together, in spite of great differences in background experience as well as, of course, language. As an *English*-speaking European, I have participated in a tendency to privilege and prioritize the English-language axis of international communication, especially transatlantic communication, to the detriment of contacts and exchanges across language barriers within Europe itself. Links formed by a common language can naturalize certain exchanges while concealing historical overdeterminations and alternatives. Maria and Giuliana's tireless skill as organizers was impressively complemented by their skill as translators and should be an inspiration to hold similar events in Britain too.

Although the theoretical references and areas of concern seemed to be shared by both groups, the Italian line of argument and aspiration are comparatively unfamiliar to English-language readers, so that reading the essays is like an experience of distanciation, strangely different but satisfyingly close to home. However, it is probably the use of feminist psychoanalysis in these essays that would present most problems to an English-speaking reader, who may well be used to a much more orthodox approach to theory. At the same time, the use of psychoanalysis may seem alienating to those who reject Freudian theory as such. It is precisely for these reasons that these essays can make a valuable contribution here. The Italian feminist theory has evolved alongside a close attention to practice and a highly politicized, militant culture. Both the *gruppi dell'inconscio* and collective textual analysis are experiments which blur a hard demarcation between theory and practice, using experience and image to draw out the contradictions inherent in women's desire. Discussion and observation are refracted through feminist politics and psychoanalytic theory to form a raw material that is comparable to the raw material of case-history. In this way issues specific to female fantasy within the context of patriarchy, that English-speaking work has tended to relegate into no-go areas as essentialist or separatist deviations, are articulated and brought to the fore.

I would like to detach one theme that runs through the essays like a coloured thread, linking different disciplines and concerns. The woman's relationship to love, or rather to the dream of love, raises particular issues for feminist theory. It offers a starting-point for understanding woman's complicity with her oppression and the force of the marginalized popular culture directed specifically at women. It is argued that fascination and pleasure generated by a binary, power-based, concept of sexual difference are not simply male and imposed from above on to the female. The dream of love is also closely connected with a child's experience of her mother (a memory that can be triggered by the image of the woman on the screen) and, indeed, with a mother's experience of her child. By analysing the problems raised by female pleasure, rather than by repressing or refusing to acknowledge its existence, it may be possible to transform or deflect it. The dream acts as a resistance to the negativity inherent in woman's binary position, so feminist politics here can take the compromised dream as a starting-point. As the dream acts as a screen for loss, sadness, and the impossibility of articulating desire or achieving reciprocity, so the cinema screen seems close to being a phantasmatic substitute. In this way, experience of the cinema, cultural or historical observation, and psychoanalytic theory combine across different disciplines, while remaining close to the touchstone of collective experience.

I would like to thank Maria Nadotti and Giuliana Bruno for organizing the conference that generated the original papers and for presenting them for an English-speaking audience; Kate Soper for translating Chapter 5, and Jude Bloomfield in association with Material Word for translating Chapters 1 and 8; Jane Armstrong at Routledge for her patience; and very particularly Rosamund Howe for help with the editing that made it possible to publish this book.

Laura Mulvey
July 1987

1 Off screen: an introduction

GIULIANA BRUNO AND MARIA NADOTTI

Translated by Jude Bloomfield in association with Material Word

A consideration of American publishing procedures reveals an obvious gap, particularly in the literature on cinema. In the United States over the last few years, a rich intellectual debate has taken place around the question of cinema. Substantive in content and in its historical and theoretical approaches, this debate has had limited contact with the work produced in other countries. Theory has moved within a more or less restricted framework with little space for translation of research work conducted outside an Anglo-American cultural perspective. In fact, the channels of communication have been confined to an interest almost exclusively focused on French theoretical writing, at the expense of a more open, free-flowing circulation of ideas. Little consideration has generally been given to Italian theory, about which little has been published, for example. The impact of what has been made available has been more or less confined to Italian specialists.

As regards cinema in particular, Italian historical and theoretical studies have largely been ignored. If we confine ourselves to the theoretical field, even today we can say that translations of historically significant and innovative research have still not appeared, for example work by Emilio Garroni with his semiotic perspective, Umberto Barbaro with his Marxist orientation, and the philosopher Galvano della Volpe, while only a very small part of the vast semiological contribution of Pier Paolo Pasolini has been translated.

This book was, therefore, conceived as a contribution to the process of documenting research projects in this area. It stems from the desire to examine aspects of Italian thought and make them known to a broader audience in an attempt to stimulate deeper and more permanent cultural exchange. Our starting-point was women's theoretical production, an area of work which particularly interests us and with which we identify. At the same time as in the United States and Britain, but largely independently, interest and studies developed in Italy which had women as their subject/object. As Italians who have been resident in New York City for several years, we were committed to disseminating to an Anglo-American audience, which was unfamiliar with it, information on the progress of research undertaken by women in Italy in an attempt to set up channels of communication and, perhaps, joint ventures.

The first step was taken in 1981. The starting-point of the project of documentation that we have undertaken, which this book is a part of, was the organization of the international conference 'Italy and the USA: the Women's Movement. A decade of feminist practice and theory', held in New York in May 1981.[1] On that occasion, Italian women involved in the field of culture and politics were invited to talk about the state of political and theoretical research in the Italian feminist movement, in a comparative exchange with their American counterparts.

From this conference, the idea emerged of organizing a more narrowly defined seminar apt to tackle a particular cultural dimension of research on women: the cinema, which lies at the heart of our common concerns. In the Women's Movement in Britain and the US over the last few years, interest in the theory of cinematic representation has developed. Problems of representation and representability of women, research on women's cinema and its implications, theorization of narrative structures, and female spectatorship are some of the approaches taken in the United States and England, to define and shape women's role in the process of film-textual production and analysis. By adopting, to a large degree, the analytic tools of semiotics and psychoanalysis, based on a critical rereading of Freud, Lacan, and post-structuralist thought, these studies have made a great contribution to the current development and revival of Anglo-American theory of cinema. This research has entered into the American academic world as a fully-fledged discipline.

Meanwhile in Italy, starting from a different perspective, a similar interest developed in the female gaze and the female voice in the cinematic apparatus. At the same time, women's participation in film production was growing in Italy as it was everywhere else. The existence and nature of this theoretical interest and practice in Italy and the results it produced were not familiar to an Anglo-American audience. We therefore thought of making them known by arranging a seminar that would provide an opportunity for comparison and exchange of our respective experiences. This book originates from the seminar at which the papers published here were given.

The seminar was held in New York in December 1984 under the title 'Italian and American directions: women's film theory and practice'.[2] We invited several Italian women involved in various capacities in the cinema world – as directors, critics or lecturers, or even just as avid and attentive spectators – to exchange opinions and research proposals with US women who were active in the same fields. It took the form of a seminar not a conference, and was conceived as a four-day workshop, centred on woman as subject/object and cinema. It seemed important to us to limit the number of participants in order to create a practical, flexible structure such as to make a genuine exchange of ideas possible. It had to work at the level which feminist practice and thought had taught us to pay particular attention to, that is the personal. We hoped to minimize the frustration that great international conferences sometimes cause by disseminating information but not providing a forum for discussion. The frequency of this kind of event had induced us to call into question the logic of the market and supermarket that lies behind the 'convention style' of some large conferences. We sought, instead, to create an open format: a workshop where differences and similarities could find expression. We wanted to promote mutual exchange between speaker and listener, giving spectatorship the active, participatory function which we were positing in theory. Such a 'dialectical' desire, so to speak, forced us to deepen our awareness of ourselves as individual and collective subjects and of the cinema-object by a meeting and comparison of our respective cultures. Therefore, we encouraged participants to present work-in-progress papers because we were interested in tracing the lines and directions of thought and the process of thinking as such, rather than in setting out results as a finished product.

Seeking to enter into the process of production of a discourse and analysing the logic of its structure also meant seeking to define and examine the relationship between film theory and practice. As well as considering women's theoretical work on cinema, recent and forthcoming examples of Italian and US film productions were shown. The four days were organized in the following way: the mornings were devoted to presentation and discussion of theoretical research, the afternoons and evenings to presentation and discussion of film and video.

In the theoretical papers we tried to touch on the complex and fundamental issues on which women have worked, to compare the theoretical orientation of Anglo-American research with that of the Italian. Despite our differences and obvious cultural and practical communication difficulties, we discovered common ground and shared methodological approaches and tools of analysis. Psychoanalysis has represented, for both sides, a fertile field of research and an important reference point in women's discourse. Interest in textual analysis and the means of representation in 'classical' Hollywood cinema compared with the 'alternative' model proposed by women's cinema proved to be another meeting-point in the discourse which has developed independently on both sides of the Atlantic. Likewise, the analysis of narrative articulation in relation to the spectator, integral to the notion of a cinematic apparatus, and the creation of subjectivity and identification, turned out to be further points of convergence.

The seminar tried to define and develop these methods and aims. Judith Mayne reviewed and analysed the key concepts proposed by Anglo-American feminist theory of cinema. Paola Melchiori, Giulia Alberti, and Adriana Monti explained the work they had carried out individually and collectively in Milan in the '150 Hours Courses'. They dealt with the various aspects of an experiment composed of theoretical and didactic work, methodological research, and film production. Laura Mulvey spoke on the development of narrative theory. She traced the theoretical advances of her position, starting from, and going beyond, the text which has become a milestone in Anglo-American discourse, 'Visual pleasure in narrative cinema' (1975).

Mary Ann Doane, Giovanna Grignaffini, and Piera Detassis gave an account of their research in progress on female spectatorship. Doane approached it from a psychoanalytic viewpoint, looking at American cinema in the 1940s, and Grignaffini and

Detassis reappropriated tools of historical analysis for their studies of Italian cinema of the 1950s. Patrizia Violi dealt with semiotic discourse in the analysis of the feminine in a contribution on language and the female subject. Lea Melandri, Lucilla Albano, and Janet Bergstrom dealt with the different aspects of psychoanalytically based research. Melandri, whose intense, theoretical research stands as a landmark in the Italian feminist movement, has played an active part in the cinema research group founded as part of the 'Training support courses for "150 Hours" teachers' in Milan. At the seminar, she set out part of her work on Sibilla Aleramo, the Italian writer whom she has redis-covered. Albano gave an example of textual analysis, inspired by a psychoanalytic model which departs from the usual reading of Freud and Lacan given in Anglo-American feminist theory. Her reading derives from Ignacio Matte Blanco's psychoanalytic theory which is based on mathematical logic. In discussing recent developments in science-fiction films, Bergstrom dealt with the problematic nature of identity and with the construction of an androgynous model. Annette Michelson examined the relationship between history, theory, and the female body in a discussion on 'The Eve of the Future' and the genealogy of the cinema. Constance Penley made a critique of the theory of the cinematic apparatus from a feminist point of view.

The seminar considered some of the aesthetic and theoretical problems and practical aspects of women's film production. We invited Shirley Clarke, Yvonne Rainer, and Susan Seidelman – three American film-makers of different generations, working in different production set-ups and with different codes – to discuss the films they were working on. They also showed us parts of their forthcoming productions.[3] The sessions devoted to show-ing Italian films and videos which had never been distributed in the USA, and recent films by British and US directors, were open to the public. Among the videos shown were those produced on the 'Training support courses for "150 Hours" teachers' in Milan by Paola Melchiori, Giulia Alberti, and Adriana Monti, 'compila-tions' that remixed and edited sequences taken from 'classical' Hollywood cinema and from films by directors like Chantal Akerman and Marguerite Duras. These deconstructed and reconstructed the complexities of female spectator fascination and the genesis of narrative desire. The video made by Annabella Miscuglio, Rony Daopoulo, and Maria Grazia Belmonti, *I fantasmi del fallo* (1980), takes up the argument of female pleasure again. This 'meta-film' consists of shooting the making of a pornographic film, superimposing, interchanging, and replacing the eye of the film-maker with that of the pornographer.

Spectatorship and psychoanalytic discourse were related in the video by Fiorella Infascelli *Ritratto di donna distesa* (1980) which gives a full-length reconstruction of a psychoanalytic session. The following were also shown: Giovanna Gagliardo's film *Maternale* (1978) which inspired a piece of Luce Irigaray's work; films and videos by Gabriella Rosaleva including *Processo a Caterina Ross* (1982) which reconstructs the last trial for witchcraft in Europe, and *Ancora una corsa* (1981) by Cinzia Torrini, a young director who has forced her way into big-budget film production. The Italian films and videos were compared with a range of recent independent productions from England and the US, including films by Bette Gordon, Laura Mulvey and Peter Wollen, Jackie Raynal, and Lynne Tillman and Sheila McLaughlin. [4]

The work presented in the field of film theory and practice prompted suggestions for the development of future research. We were confronted with the current assumption of a negative aesthetic and we discussed possible ways of overcoming it. The question of female identity as *other*, as the negative pole, was raised; also the definition of female specificity through the metaphor of absence, lack and non-being, and the construction of the female subject through a work of deconstruction of dominant, phallogocentric discourse. We discussed how the negative aesthetic and theory could be developed, or whether it was necessary to abandon it, and, if so, how. It was pointed out that feminist practice has long focused on the question of the representation and image of woman in the cinema. This work, as it has gone beyond the phase of iconography, has pointed to the need to look at the female body as the phantasmatic ground of cinema itself. Interest was reawakened in investigating the narrative and spectator devices with new means, trying to arrive at a definition of the 'contemplative gaze' in cinema. A hypothetical return to a pre-Oedipal phase was proposed as a means of interpreting female spectator fascination, and a hypothesis on the androgyny of the spectator was formulated. Concepts were put forward to enhance feminist film theory, going beyond semiotics and psychoanalysis to focus on film history and the problem of its theorization.

We both believed that 'verba volant, scripta manent' ('while the spoken word flies, the written word remains'). The various voices which asked us to record the experience of the seminar in some way, to make the research work of Italian women available to those who were not there, and offer contributors the opportunity to sum up and draw some conclusions, were in agreement with us. This anthology is the outcome. It brings together the Italian contributions to the seminar, sets them in context, and adds hitherto unpublished material and information about the activities of women in Italy who are involved in film and video. It is aimed at English-language readers with an interest in cinema, women's issues, and contemporary Italian culture.

In order to clarify further the context where the texts here published were produced, it may be useful, at this point, to place them within the political and theoretical framework of Italian feminism. In the following pages, we will attempt to outline and analyse some points of similarity and difference between the Anglo-American and the Italian experience. We will stress the strong political edge of Italian feminist research and its very particular interpretation of psychoanalysis, towards a definition of a 'political unconscious'.

Throughout the 1970s Italy witnessed an explosive growth and proliferation of collective practice and experimentation. Feminism played a prominent part in this process, which sought to establish new forms of political practice and knowledge. A central principle for these 'movements' was that political practice is a form of knowledge and that the act of knowing, as well as its theorization, implies a political positioning. The traditional language of political discourse was called into question. In order to convey new meanings, new structures and forms were sought.

Italian feminism was experimenting with a political practice closely linked to a female experience of knowledge, both individual and collective. It grew within a logic, the centre of which was the small group. With the help of psychoanalysis, feminism developed a political group practice of continual analysis and self-analysis, questioning subjectivity, identity, sexual difference, and pleasure. Such was the premise of many consciousness-raising groups and of the *gruppi dell'inconscio*. The *gruppi dell'inconscio* were groups specifically aimed at exploring the working of the unconscious – members' dreams and fantasies.

The political experience of knowledge and self-knowledge

carried through in the form of the small group resisted centralization. The small group is a 'centrifugal centre' of dissemination of
discourse, where knowledge and self-knowledge are articulated
and realized in the form of political commitment and experience.
Such experiences were varied and multi-faceted, full of nuances,
highly specific and individual in character, and in a state of continual progress and flux. They confront History with both the
strength and the weakness of the insurgence of micro-histories,
of 'savoirs mineurs', of local knowledges, of specific and
repressed voices in which sexuality and the unconscious emerge
in all their 'differance', distinctiveness, and diversity. It was
rarely possible or desirable to capitalize on the wealth and subtlety
of achievements and discoveries that are often visible and comprehensible only to the direct participants, to make them visible
outward, permanent or even simply to put them on record.

Therein lies the peculiarity of the Italian situation. In Italy, the
Women's Movement, just like the mode of discourse it has produced, has not engaged in a struggle to carve out a space for itself
in the given institutions of knowledge. It has travelled through
more uneven and uncertain paths, in a constant state of questioning, ambivalence towards gaining power and status, and
acquiring recognition. In the subtle play between power and
knowledge, Italian feminism was strengthened by the force of
the inventiveness of its deviant, oppositional discourse, which
seemed to make separation preferable to confrontation, negotia-
tion with the institution, and possible compromise. By the same
token, it was weakened by its own constant self-questioning.
The preoccupation with self-analysis which characterized feminist process and strategy, and which was the strength of its form
of discourse, was also the locus of its weakness. A political discourse underlined by a desire to break into the unconscious was
found to disperse, leaving behind only the most solitary, secret,
and individual traces.

Therefore, the forms of discourse proposed in this anthology
are to be considered as the tip of the iceberg, that is, as what has
come to the surface as formalized texts from a rich trajectory of
research that the concern with the unconscious has made 'invisible'. They are what emerged in highly codified form from
equally, perhaps more significant, extensive informal manifestations of discourse. These texts thus acquire sense as a limited system of presences in an oral history, in the complex articulation

and distribution of the 'unspoken' which characterizes Italian feminist discourse and strategy. Within this 'invisible' articulation and circulation, our own work of documentation is to be positioned.

Without claiming to be exhaustive or to offer the reader the whole range of the Italian discourse, we are proposing one of the many possible manifestations and readings, an area less resistant to textual formalization. To grasp the Italian experience one should be aware that it is different from what produced 'Women's Studies', the experience of knowledge which has played and still plays such a major part in the direction of women's intellectual and political research in the United States. The path pursued by American feminism, that of acquiring the status of a formal discipline, a field of 'scholarship', a path which has generated 'feminist film theory', has no parallel in Italy where feminist theory and criticism are not identified in the same way as an academic field or option. Italian feminist discourse does not function as accumulation of knowledge, as its *modus operandi* is a practice of dissemination. This is not to say that there are no feminists in academia but rather that the phenomenon of a feminist academia in Italy does not exist. Research is often more solitary, less identified or identifiable with a position, theoretical or otherwise; there are fewer traceable parallels between projects, which have stronger links with non-academic settings. The papers that we present here cannot be seen as the Italian equivalent of American 'feminist film theory' since they are the result of research which has developed neither inside nor outside academia but traversing a space in between.

Perhaps this is part of the novelty and interest of Italian women's theoretical production and practice in the field of film studies. We are dealing with a discourse which sought to avoid the split in representation between the intellectual and the political, academia and activism, the public and the private, and which often arose precisely to overcome such divisions. The resistance to such binary oppositions is not only a feature of women's production but is a broader phenomenon which can be attributed to the general nature of Italian culture and its forms of organization. There is no rigid distinction between the academic and other domains, nor are there rigid distinctions between their different forms and channels of discourse. The Women's Movement, like every other political movement in Italy, is engaged in positing theoretical questions; vice versa, traditionally in Italian thought, theoretical investigation is not divorced from political and social praxis. The creation and development of such thought, including thinking on the cinema, have followed paths which are related, above all, to historic forms of alternative political organization and to a particular use of psychoanalysis, within a process of redefinition and reappropriation of interpretative tools.

The dramatic growth of feminism in Italy historically followed, was generated within, and, at the same time, set to surpass the massive political movement of 1968, of which feminism was a subversive product. Consequently the confrontation with Marxism, with both Marxist theory and political praxis, was more painful for Italian women and was undertaken as an unavoidable commitment. For many, militancy in a political party of the traditional Left, the Communist Party or in the New Left groups (Il Manifesto, Lotta Continua, Avanguardia Operaia, etc.) had been the first step to 'emancipation'. At the beginning, feminism represented a dual militancy. The break with the political groupings to consolidate independent forms of organization and thought was made with great difficulty and extreme ambivalence towards the notion of political organization itself, a notion continually put into question by feminists.

Inside a framework of small, uncentralized groups, both consciousness-raising groups and *gruppi dell'inconscio*, women became involved in examining the type of relations which are formed within social and political organizations as they relate to the question of power. The first theoretical break brought about by Italian feminism was, therefore, the analysis of relations of power and domination in social and political structures, starting from the family and going all the way to the leftist groups, in order to reach definition of female identity, subjectivity, and pleasure. This process of research followed a path which began with, and traversed, Marxism, and naturally led to reaching and traversing psychoanalysis.

Within this process, Italian feminism has vacillated between separatist opposition to dominant culture, and attempts at insertion, maybe for the sake of survival. This experience has generated over 100 women's study centres, organizations where intellectual research is linked to the personal and the political, that are alternative to, and generally separated from, the official institutions of knowledge.[5] Some of the writings presented here were produced in such settings. Giovanna Grignaffini's text forms part of the work in progress being carried out at the Women's Research and Documentation Centre in Bologna. Annabella Miscuglio's contribution is that of a film-maker involved in a feminist film production collective. The texts written by Alberti, Melandri, Melchiori, and Monti, derived, as has been mentioned, from their shared experience in the '150 Hours Courses' in Milan. We wanted to highlight this important and original experience, which is unlike any in the Anglo-American context. It is described in our afterword to the four Milanese contributions entitled 'On the margins of feminist discourse: the experience of the "150 Hours Courses"'.

As can be seen in the Milanese texts, despite the differences, feminist research in Italy, like its Anglo-American counterpart, has turned to psychoanalysis as the privileged territory of analysis. However, the reference to psychoanalysis reveals a different trajectory and different treatment of sources. Italian feminism relates more to Freud's writings than to the Lacanian interpretation which has attracted greater interest among Anglo-American women. Within Freudian theory, Italian interest has focused on the pre-Oedipal phase. Furthermore, it is worth stressing that in Italy psychoanalysis has become one of the principal means of women's investigation of the cinematic text and apparatus, not as much for its academic interest, but as a result of its rooted presence in the forms of theoretical questioning and political practice of feminism. The reference is inscribed in a continuous line of development, ranging from the historical practice of consciousness-raising groups and *gruppi dell'inconscio* to the definition of objective areas. This point, which we expand on in our 'Editors' introduction' to the texts of Melchiori, Alberti, Melandri, and Monti, concerns the positioning and articulation of psychoanalytic discourse in Italian feminism.

In general, the use of Freudian psychoanalysis forms part of an almost linear progression which started off with the Women's Movement practice, its interest in, and subtle and refined ability to investigate the self, identity, and subjectivity. Gradually this spread to wider and wider areas of experience, including, and focusing on, the female experience of pleasure. In the definition of objective fields of analysis, the premise remained constant that knowledge and inventiveness arise solely from the ability to see by looking at oneself, and hear by listening to one's own voice. A fluid relationship between the inner and the outer, the self and the other, was sought. In the experience of collective textual analysis, which has played an important role in women's intellectual trajectory in Italy, theoretical analysis and self-analysis were acting upon transference, acting clinically, establishing new relations among and for women, and opening up the field of pleasure. To convey the originality of Italian feminist work, one could say that it resides in an unusual, unorthodox, but not inappropriate use of the psychoanalytic mode. Italian feminism has challenged a classical polarization, the dichotomy between psychoanalysis as theory on the one hand or as therapy on the other. It has reappropriated the Freudian psychoanalytic mode, as a unitary, clinical-theoretical process, affirming the theoretical potential of the clinical tool. Practising theory acts as a means of enquiry into identity and the relation to the Symbolic, in the belief that theory is not split off from or other than self; nor does it function simply as a methodology to be applied to an object.

Consciously questioning the split, at a particular point in the history of feminist analysis, women's gaze turns from themselves to the cinema. A kind of inversion of terms takes place, in which the person analysing and reading the filmic text is, at the same time, read and worked through, in a theoretical-clinical process. The female subject, recognizing herself as such, casts upon her object a look off screen, a look of presence and absence, internal and external, allusive and pregnant as the off screen space is. Such a look problematizes the object in problematizing the subject. That is why in Italy we started off so insistently with the problematics of female spectatorship rather than with the question of textual representation. Discourse on female fascination and desire precedes analysis of representation, and questions are asked not only about the relationship between knowledge and power but also and especially about their link with female pleasure. This is also evident, and enhanced, in the practice of the Italian feminist film production which we showed at the seminar.

Here Italian feminism makes an important contribution as it theoretically dwells on the figure of the mother. Anglo-Saxon feminism often regards pleasure as a projection of the male gaze. Analysis of the experience of pleasure in cinema has substantially concentrated its efforts in deconstructing it, as a process triggered by the male. The position of Italian feminism affirms,

and opens a space for, female pleasure. It acknowledges its problematic nature, rather than denying it as simply imposed upon
women by male-dominated discourse. In the insistence upon the
'dream of love' (*il sogno d'amore*) and fascination which we find in
the Italian texts, we recognize interesting suggestions for further
theoretical development. The relation between dominant/
oppressed is conceived as something more than and different
from a clear-cut binary opposition. One cannot simply speak of
reflection of dominant discourse as regards the oppressed; even
a mirror distorts. In the passage, in the transition from dominant
to oppressed, something happens. It is an instance of trans/form-
ation, not simply a collapse of one on to the other. Precisely
within such space, in the compromised space of that 'transference' which occurs in female spectatorship, if nowhere else, we
may find a starting-point to reverse negativity and negation of
female pleasure. In this sense, female pleasure is acknowledged
a space in the process of representation not simply as the obscure
object of desire, a shadow of the desire of the other. And so is her
pleasure recognized as a complex site, indeed of (re)appropriation,
but also subversion of male-constructed discourse and gaze.
Acknowledging the activity of female pleasure, its autonomy, we
can reconsider the theoretical and political space of pleasure itself.
Otherwise, despite all intentions, and for a perverse twist, feminism risks contributing in a moralizing politics of negation of
pleasure. The acknowledgement of female pleasure engages in a
line of enquiry upon the complexity of the relation between politics
and theory, dominant and oppressed, male and female, active and
passive, seeing and being seen, representing and being represented. Such complexity of relations, for example, is inscribed in
the very theoretical foundations of the 'dream of love', the problematic of the dream-screen and the clinical-theoretical perspective,
raised by a number of the texts published here.

These are some of the implications of the priority given by Italian feminist studies to the question of fascination and female
desire. As regards cinema, enquiry takes as a starting-point the
point of view of the female who is engaged in the activity of criticism. It poses the question of her own pleasure in the attempt to
grasp the relationship between the spectator's gaze and critical-
scientific scrutiny. This perspective, positioned as if it were
off screen, continually inverts the relationship of seeing and
been seen, analysed object and analysing subject, analyst and

analysand. Out of these critical initiatives and efforts, a solid and stimulating body of theoretical work has taken shape in Italy, albeit in a fragmented, uneven patchwork of different approaches. We wanted to give a sample of the variety of experiences rather than a unified picture, providing a survey that covers some aspects of Italian critical theory and film practice.

The papers that follow, rather than as autonomous texts, for the most part signify as an integral part of a whole structure of discourse and of the specific context in which they were produced. They ask the reader to temporarily suspend judgement on their own textual status and autonomy. In this way, a 'body' of work, that is *de facto* transformed into disembodied voices by the written word and by the very process of documenting, selecting, and isolating, may be returned to the reader. The textual pleasure of the written word does not include or convey the pleasure experienced at the seminar where the papers were produced, a pleasure which was predicated upon the energy of a bodily presence, a physical excitement of being and thinking together, an important part of the feminist experience. The female authors, their corporate presence, must die, in the Barthesian sense, for their texts to be born. As individual texts, they have been dismembered from a larger, often 'invisible' body of work, and from the *esprit de corps*, the solidarity and consciousness of a collective body which feminist discourse, in its political import, embodies.

Although we have pursued a different path and have reached a different position from that of current American feminist film theory, the points and themes we have arrived at are very similar to those which British and US women are interested in. The questions we have formulated are also central to Anglo-Saxon research. Often the choice of methodology and the results of research reveal a common interest in certain critical language and interpretative tools. Those which occupy a privileged place are semiotics, textual analysis, and psychoanalysis. In documenting work in this field, it seems to us important to point out not only the difference but also the convergence in formulation and frames of reference. These tell us something about the specificity and also the universality of feminist discourse. Those who have worked in an Anglo-American environment will recognize the complex problems and real points at issue which are being continually grappled with on the Italian side as well. Obviously it is no accident, and it may be worth asking why certain discourses recur. Recognizing them, as one recognizes oneself as the other in the screen-mirror of identification, could be the first step to understanding and transcending a theoretical impasse, defining and overcoming it. In this sense, without claiming to offer miraculous solutions or reformulations, as a work of documentation, this book simply invites the reader to look at the other as reflection of self, in the hope that the process will not stop there.

NOTES

1 The conference 'Italy and the USA: the Women's Movement. A decade of feminist practice and theory' was conceived and orga- nized by Maria Nadotti for the New York University Program of French and Italian Studies, and by Marilyn Young and Molly Nolan for the History Department of New York University. The conference was jointly sponsored by the University and by the Italian Institute of Culture in New York. It was held from 28 to 30 May 1981 and marked a moment of intense and lively exchange of information and experiences.

   Divided into four sessions on different themes, and workshops and discussion groups, the conference dealt with the experience of the Italian and North American feminist movements, through the themes of *health, violence against women, culture, consciousness and women's organization within the trade union and party structures.*

   For Italy, the following people spoke: Bimba De Maria (journal- ist), Chiara Ingrao (representative of the CGL (General Confedera- tion of Italian Labour)), Dacia Maraini (writer), Luisa Morgantini (representative of the FLM (Metalworkers Federation)), Luisa Muraro (University of Verona, feminist theorist and co-ordinator of the *Libreria delle Donne* in Milan), Carla Pasquinelli (University of Cagliari), Franca Pizzini (University of Milan, GRIFF (Research Group on Women and the Family)), Gabriella Rossetti (University of Ferrara, Milan co-ordinator of the 'Training support groups for "150 Hours" teachers' since 1974), Loredana Rotondo (film-maker, co-director of *Processo per stupro* which was shown at the confer- ence), Chiara Saraceno (University of Trento), and Micki Staderini (co-founder and mentor of the Virginia Woolf Centre in Rome).

   For the United States the following people contributed: Judy Andler (Transition House), Angela Autera (Pennsylvania Coalition against Domestic Violence), Ros Baxandall (*Feminist Studies*, SUNY Old Westbury), Boston Women's Health Collective, Wendy Chav- kin (consultant on Reproductive Hazards in the Workplace), Cindy Chin (Massachusetts Battered Women's Shelter Coalition), Barbara

Ehrenreich (Institute for the Humanities, New York University), Mary Elgin (United States Workers of America), Liz Ewen (SUNY Old Westbury), P. Catlin Fullwood (public education specialist), Alice Kessler Harris (Hofstra University, *Feminist Studies*, District 65, Labor College), Freada Klein (Alliance against Sexual Coercion, HAWC (Help for Abused Women and Children), Margaret Kovak (Prudence Crandall Shelter for Battered Women), Rape Crisis Centre Washington, DC), Rayna Rapp (*Feminist Studies*, New School for Social Research), Susan Schechter (Park Slope Safe Home Project), Belinda Sifford (CARUSA (Committee for Abortion Rights and against Sterilization Abuse)), Catherine Stimpson (Rutgers University, *Signs* former editor).

2. The seminar 'Italian and American directions: women's film theory and practice' was held in New York at New York University, The Kitchen, and the Italian Cultural Institute from 6 to 9 December 1984.

Among the participants were: Lucilla Albano (Florence University), Giulia Alberti (Albedo, Milan), Judith Barry (filmmaker), Fina Bathrick (Hunter College), Janet Bergstrom (University of California, Los Angeles, and *Camera Obscura*), Yvette Biro (New York University), Joan Braderman (School of Visual Arts), Iris Cahn (film-maker), Shirley Clarke (film-maker), Joan Copjec (*October*), Teresa de Lauretis (University of California, Santa Cruz), Piera Detassis (*Cinema e Cinema*), Mary Ann Doane (Brown University), Lucy Fischer (University of Pittsburgh), Sandy Flitterman (Rutgers University), Ann Friedberg (University of California, Irvine), Giovanna Gagliardo (film-maker), Bette Gordon (film-maker), Giovanna Grignaffini (Bologna University), Deedee Halleck (TV programme producer), E. Ann Kaplan (Rutgers University), Marjorie Keller (film-maker), Mary Kelly (artist), Sheila McLaughlin (filmmaker), Judith Mayne (Ohio State University), Lea Melandri (theorist), Patricia Mellencamp (University of Wisconsin, Milwaukee), Paola Melchiori (Gervasia Broxon co-op, Milan), Annette Michelson (New York University and *October*), Annabella Miscuglio (filmmaker), Adriana Monti (film-maker and Albedo, Milan), Laura Mulvey (film-maker and theorist), Constance Penley (University of Rochester and *Camera Obscura*), Yvonne Rainer (film-maker), Jackie Raynal (film-maker and programmer), Ruby Rich (New York State Council for the Arts), Gabriella Rosaleva (film-maker), Mary Russo (Hampshire College), Susan Seidelman (film-maker), Kaja Silverman (Simon Fraser University), Abigail Solomon-Godeau (International Center of Photography), Janet Staiger (New York University), Jennifer Stone (University of Massachusetts, Amherst), Amy Taubin (film-maker and programmer), Lynne Tillman (film-maker and writer), Maureen Turim (SUNY, Binghamton), Patrizia Violi (Bologna University), Jane Weinstock (film-maker and theorist).

3 *Ornette/Made in America* by Shirley Clarke, *The Man who Envied Women* by Yvonne Rainer, and *Desperately Seeking Susan* by Susan Seidelman, all three in the production phase in 1984.
4 *Variety* (1983) by Bette Gordon, *Frida and Tina* (1983) by Laura Mulvey and Peter Wollen, *Hotel New York* (1983) by Jackie Raynal, and *Committed* (1984) by Lynne Tillman and Sheila McLaughlin.
5 We can cite as examples of these the Virginia Woolf Centre in Rome, the only Italian experiment in an alternative women's university; the *Libreria delle Donne* in Milan, an influential centre of political-theoretical production; the Sibilla Aleramo Centre in Milan, attached to the Feltrinelli Institute; the 'Intercategoriale donne' (Women's Melting Pot') in Turin; the Women's Centre in Pisa; and the 'Women's Archive' in Naples.

The most recent publications include: P. Melchiori (ed.) (1987) *Verifica d'identità. Materiali, esperienze, riflessioni sul fare cultura tra donne*, Rome: Utopia; A. Cavarero et al. (1987) *Diotima: il pensiero della differenza sessuale*, Milan: La Tartaruga; and Libreria della donne (1987) *Non credere di avere dei diritti*, Turin: Rosenberg & Sellier.

PART I

The '150 Hours'

2 Editors' introduction

GIULIANA BRUNO AND MARIA NADOTTI

Translated by Rosamund Howe

As stated in 'Off screen: an introduction', the chapters by Paola Melchiori, Giulia Alberti, Lea Melandri, and Adriana Monti were all written against the same political and cultural background: the '150 Hours Courses'. Its political implications are discussed in 'On the margins of feminist discourse: the experience of the "150 Hours Courses"', which is an afterword to the four chapters. Here we would like to stress the origin of the psychoanalytic discourse which informs it.

The four chapters all refer to a political and cultural experiment which was centred in Milan at the beginning of the 1970s but which subsequently became a part of the heritage and a distinctive practice of the entire Italian Women's Movement: the exploration of the unconscious.

From the beginning of the Italian feminist movement women in consciousness-raising groups had practised self-analysis, albeit in a descriptive and superficial way; they had thus arrived on to uncharted ground, half-way between psychoanalysis and politics. Improvised autobiographies were readily assimilated into collective thought within an informal group structure. But it was the new phenomenon of deepening friendship between women, which was granted the same importance as theoretical research into sexuality and the body, that provided the impetus for a radical project, that of the *pratica dell'inconscio*, the exploration of the unconscious; this practice

was to give the feminist movement an autonomy and specificity
of its own, clearly demarcating it from the psychoanalytic tradition and known political modes.

An article written by a Milanese collective ('Alcune femministe
milanesi') entitled 'Pratica dell'inconscio e movimento delle
donne' ('Exploration of the unconscious and the Women's Movement') was published in the magazine *L'erba voglio* (1974–5). It
discussed the need to devise a group practice to confront a 'specific discourse of the unconscious', that which is revealed in the
stories women tell about themselves and, particularly, in their
complex and unexplored relationships with each other. The
mother-daughter relationship, as located in the experience of the
groups and relived through the increasingly intense emotional,
sexual, and intellectual relations in them, brought new confirmation to the intuition that woman does not exist as a separate and
different category. This focused members' attention on the
'invisible violence' which keeps them trapped in an illusory
identity, built on the body of another, quite unconsciously and in
the interests of survival. All the well-known polarizations can be
seen behind the male and female: internal-external, individual-
collective, body-mind, etc. The image of the double aspect, the
coming together of two poles which men, throughout history,
have wanted to keep divided and counterposed, is not yet so
apparent or so detached from how women feel and think as to
allow a union between the dualism which shapes the whole of
culture and the 'dream of love', and between the myth of the
Androgyne and the nostalgia for an original oneness modelled
on the male prototype. The exploration of the unconscious dis-
places from the theoretical and professional institution of psychoanalysis on to a political terrain the legitimacy of a form of
knowledge which investigates the space between words and behaviour in similar ways to case histories. It throws light on the images,
loved and hated, seductive and troubling, with which women
look at themselves but fail to see themselves, products of male
fantasy but none the less significant for women's psychic life.

In the initial stage, out of the need to construct a form of knowledge which could take account of sexual difference and could
also actually modify it, an original practice began to develop.
It acted upon 'transference' fantasies without assigning roles,
and interpreted arguing with established theories when new
discoveries so required, but was nevertheless in some ways

reminiscent of a clinical practice. The second stage revealed the need to find connections between the life of sexuality and the emotions and the whole accumulation of interests, loves, and work which make up each individual's experience. This gave rise to new groups such as Women and Writing, Women and Cinema, and Women and Work; these demonstrated that a working method was developing, capable of unexpected rigour and originality with respect to traditional 'scientific methodology' and capable of articulation on various different levels: research, professionalism, institutional languages, etc. These groups avoided the division between study and cultural specialization on the one hand, and the personal (emotions, dreams, survival, etc.) on the other, which arises on account of the difficulty of analysing oneself and one's relationships. The practice of exploration of the unconscious prevented this split and challenged the division of knowledge into separate spheres: public/private, social/personal. Participants were able to study the fantasies, emotions, displacements, and attributions of meanings with which they approached an object of love, a person, a language, a text, by catching themselves in the act; consequently, their behaviour could be acted on with all the effectiveness of therapy, and also through a new form of social relations between women.

The following four chapters took shape in the ambit of this project. Those by Melchiori and Alberti concentrate particularly on identity, identification, and fascination in the cinema in relation to the problematic of the 'dream' and the illusion of perfection and unity. They emphasize the pre-Oedipal stage of identification with the mother.

Lea Melandri's chapter records a stage in an original theoretical-clinical psychoanalytic formulation on the 'dream of love', which reappears in the collective enquiry into women and cinema in which she was one of the participants. The work on the 'dream of love' should be seen in the context of the general interest taken in the subject of 'love' by European psychoanalytic theorists (see for example Julia Kristeva's work on 'tales of love', in particular *Histoires d'amour* (1983) and the writings on the 'ethic of passions' of Luce Irigaray, notably *Ethique de la différance sexuelle* (1985)). Melandri's work is an important reference-point in Italian feminism. Compared with other Milanese texts, Melandri's differs in its method of work and writing as well as in its content. She reached her theory of the 'dream of love' through the rediscovery of the Italian writer Sibilla Aleramo (1878–1960). Melandri articulates her own discourse through that of another woman. Aleramo's writing takes on the function of subtext, to be read and rewritten at the same time, in a symbiotic process which goes beyond citation and admits neither dependency nor disembodiment. Thus the 'dream of love' is not only the object of the writing but also articulates its form.

Finally we present the script of Adriana Monti's film *Scuola senza fine*, a film project generated within the political-cultural context of the Milanese group.

3 Women's cinema: A look at female identity

PAOLA MELCHIORI

Translated by Jane Dolman

Feminist critics have put a great deal of thought into analysing classical cinema and images of woman's body as 'object of the look'. But as film-makers, women become the *subjects* of the look. When a woman becomes the one who looks, what image of her sexual identity does she reflect? How does she go beyond the representations and identities of her unconscious conditioning as mother or sexual object?

Beyond an over-facile conflation of the acquisition of language with the acquisition of subjectivity, the forms and figurations of the female body that emerge out of 'freedom of expression', and the meaning at stake in the activity of self-representation, can now become objects of an analysis that can finally dispense with the terms used hitherto, such as 'unfreedom of the victim' and the 'figuration of oppression'.

A FEW HYPOTHESES

The miracle resided wholly in the fact that she was outside of me and not inside, she was not the projection of my dream or my anguish but something autonomous, beyond my imagination – I wasn't dreaming her, I wasn't singing her, she was not in my heart, she was in my room.

(Tsvetaeva 1982; my translation)

Women's cinema, or indeed any existential or symbolic action by a woman, can only be considered in the context of the construction and complexity of *desire*, which is the only source for the formulation of an *image*, leaving aside, that is, possible forms that relations between women, or between one woman and herself, assume either in reality or in the symbolic, in history or in a world based on the polarization of the male and female as opposition and complementarity. The cinema therefore gives women the possibility of representing themselves in such a way that their own bodies, their own individual beings, defined and sexed, can be looked at and recognized without being subsumed into a need or idealized into a dream. It offers the hope of finding something similar to Freud's concept of the *heimlich*. To achieve this, however, it is essential to be able to face and deal with forces that oppose this hope, forces that are not so much outside as inside the woman herself. To use the provocative, disturbing words of Otto Weininger, a man whose 'horror of the female' gave him a clear perception of many aspects of the feminine: 'The greatest, the one enemy of the emancipation of women is woman herself' (1906: 75) and 'will woman choose to abandon slavery in order to become unhappy?' (1906: 348).

The view of women's cinema presented here will not endorse a new image or language, but will examine the obstacles along a slow and hazardous course seeking how woman may approach both herself and other women, real women, not magnified out of proportion by demand or dream, in order to establish the possible existence of symbolic activity that can harmonize with her own and others' femininity. The result would be to overcome the split in our being that Virginia Woolf often spoke about:

> Why, she reflected, should there be this perpetual disparity between the thought and the action . . . this astonishing precipice on one side of which the soul was active and in broad daylight, on the other side of which it was contemplative and as dark as night? (Woolf 1971: 358)

We have now gone beyond the stage of discovering and vindicating a 'difference' or, as Luce Irigaray described it, *otherness* and *innocence* and having to draw a boundary between woman's world and man's retreating from the horror and violence of the male world. We need now to investigate the *complicity* and *mimesis* of desire, the fundamental reasons for woman's attachment to the world and to the images and relations that have condemned her historically and existentially.

It is no coincidence that women's most usual relationship with their own image and the symbolic world is particularly clearly visible in film. In the concealed but identifiable presence of the camera, the cinema foregrounds the primal transformation process that lies behind all symbolic activity, that lies behind language but becomes invisible within it. This is the relation between body and sense that is half-way between metonymy and metaphor, between Barthes's 'obtuseness' of the body and the 'pleasure of the text', between the intractability of feelings and their elaboration in language, in its ability, for instance, to transform 'pure anguish' into the grief of bereavement. The cinema reproduces both the subject of desire and the subject of language, the unliveable world of feelings and the civilized world of culture. As in learning and working experiences, where the earliest associations that children attach to the presence of their mother return to haunt women's relationships with each other in the face of culture, so in the cinema does the representation of the female body on the screen recall the very early figurations and symbolizations that lie behind the everyday actions of life and of language.

I will, therefore, speak of 'women's cinema' as an aspect of women's relationship with their own image, and of this image as the primary form of symbolization.

The analysis could take two different directions which, in the specific case of women's cinema, appear to converge. In the case of the woman as director we could try to understand how her creative work as narrator, of producing film, is unconsciously influenced by the fact of her being female, given that her own body, the image of her identity, faces her on the screen as image, as object of the look, as 'impossible' body.

In the case of the woman spectator we could try to see how the 'normal' mechanisms of primary and secondary identification take different forms when the camera is in the hands of a female subject, and duplicates the female spectator's gaze at the screen.

In this essay there are no specific references to films, but two women directors, Chantal Akerman and Margarethe Von Trotta, were constantly in my mind. The difference usually noted between their films is in their use of an experimental and a classical language respectively. But I regard this as secondary to their 'figuration of the feminine' which is an important motif in the work of both directors.

COMPLICITY IN THE DREAM OF PERFECTION

'The essence of the image is . . . without signification yet summoning upon the depth of any possible meaning; unrevealed yet manifest, having that absence-as-presence which constitutes the lure and the fascination of the sirens' (M. Blanchot, quoted in Barthes 1984: 106).

As the ultimate triumph of the image, the cinema also makes the most extreme statement of woman's ontological constitution as dream and illusion for the other.

In Kierkegaard's words:

> For what is woman but a dream? – and yet she is the highest reality? So it is the erotic understands her and leads her and is led by her at the moment of seduction – outside of time where she belongs as an illusion in her own place . . . . But this illusion is precisely the calamity . . . inasmuch as she can never free herself from the illusion with which life has consoled her. . . . For all her identity is illusion . . . . Thus woman has a possibility such as no man has . . . but her reality is in inverse proportion to that and the most dreadful thing of all is the sorcery of illusion in which she feels happy. (Kierkegaard 1940)

These words give voice to the other face of the feminine, which the familiar figuration of the 'downtrodden' victim conceals, that is the *complicity* between male and female desire, even in enmity. It is this element that allows 'classical' cinematic analysis of woman as object of male voyeurism not to deny the female gaze but to locate a *confusion* of the male's look-desire with that of the female.

There is a primal problem, common to both men and women, that generates the illusion of seeing the infinite in the limited and concrete, of projecting perfection, unattainable by any single individual, on to a complementary other, in a mechanism that underlies concepts of the sacred, love, and male-female polarity. This problem is shared by men and women alike, but the possibility of expressing it varies for each sex.

In male fantasy the woman's body as object does not only signify the fetishistic 'Oedipal' body; it is also the body as site of primal perfection, the *ideal body* of pre-sexual beauty, the unified body of the myth of the 'Uroborus'.[1] Freud posits a splitting mechanism at the origin of religiosity and of fetishism. This mechanism denies, in order to conserve, both the perception of reality and the child's earliest desires, thus constituting a split in the first object and leaving the subject lacerated in an irreducible duality and ambivalence.

The construction of the fetish makes it possible to deny the mother's castration. But before she is perceived sexually as a castration threat, the mother signifies difference, and difference signifies a separation, the loss of that world of fusion, the specular mother-son co-identity, which, long before the 'Oedipal phantasy of possessing the mother', characterizes the disturbing bliss of infancy, an 'ecstatic' place where the child is mother and son, man and woman, one and the other, an *omnipotent child-god* who has not yet been forced to choose to differentiate itself and limit its sexual identity.

Unable to go on being the mother, a man will try to possess her. For those who accede to the sexual norm, the maternal Double, the Specular Other on the threshold between Male and Female becomes 'the object of desire'. The 'oceanic feeling' of identification is transformed into an 'object relation', and the ecstasy of 'being one' fragments into the discontent of possession.[2]

The feminine aspect of this early identification with the mother has to be split off and expelled. It returns from outside, laden with nostalgia and the threat of seduction, personified in Woman, in the Sacred, in the figures underlying the phenomenon of religiosity, in Freud's sense of the term.

Thus, for a man, behind the trivial brutality of sexual objectivization, the ideal of the specular ego persists, a beautiful mother-sister-twin, lost in a world 'overshadowed by ancient dreams' (Musil 1979). The idealized beauty of classical (cinematic, literary, etc.) representation of the feminine contains an ancient *ideal ego*, that coexists with the partial object formed later by fetishization.

What is less evident is that the woman has to face the same fundamental problem, although the outcome is not the same. An equally powerful desire to deny separation, loss, and emptiness, to maintain a belief in maternal omnipotence, either real or imaginary, is the constitutive factor in both male and female desire, which are, in the first instance, similar.

Before a woman assumes the sexual identification that forces her to choose between her objectivization as female and 'absolute subjectivity' as mother, she has experienced an ideal place, a pre-sexual, infantile territory that is tenaciously dreamed of, although lost.

But while a man has the possibility of inventing the maternal-female, the image of castration is imposed on a woman, before her sense of loss can find any means of expression, so that she is left with only defensive, secondary elaborations. Her defence against desire for the other tends to become confused with the desire to conserve intact her infantile dream of Omnipotent Totality; and her dream is as strong as, and the same as, the dream that drives man to invent the female.

If woman is denied the real satisfaction of perpetual possession of the maternal body, symbolically and in reality, her only satisfaction can be in frustrated desire, an ecstasy similar to that of mysticism. If man can rediscover the mother-woman in daydreams which also become real in night-time illusion, female 'reality' can only be found in the dreams of sleep. If she is unable to live, she can wait and dream. An active attempt to preserve desire intact is concealed in an inversion, in the passivity to which femininity is destined.

To counter the fulfilment of male narcissism, woman builds an empty fortress, a narcissistic castle in which she can even more violently reject the realities, constraints, and vicissitudes of actual relationships. To counter the painful interruption of the temporality of real desire, her time will be mystical, eternal. A superillusion will arise to counter the illusion.

A façade of servitude is therefore a defence. It actively resists giving up the 'total dream' that is connected to an omnipotent female figure.

In servitude, powerlessness hides a fantastic ability to embody total otherness, a pretended negation of the maternal hides control and possession of the other; silence veils what is longing to be revealed. The impossibility of reality becomes the 'certainty' of dream. To incarnate, in this way, the 'eternal illusion' demanded by the other also demands loyalty to her own childhood dream.

Idealization of the male, which has a different meaning but a similar form, becomes confused with, and gives refuge to, the persistent dream of a child-woman. This illusion veils the most obvious evidence of oppression and, perhaps, goes some way to explain why women are the world's 'only slaves who love their chains' (Bocchetti).

If, therefore, man's ambivalence (which takes the dual form of idealization and execration) is towards a bond which he would like to be both eternal and severed, towards a freedom which he both fears and desires, then woman's ambivalence (which takes the form of misery and omnipotence) can result in nothing more than deception and disappointment, as if it were impossible to get close to oneself or to another woman without the presence of an omnipotent, idealized figure. The self-confidence which women represent for each other at the start of 'the journey of life' often turns into a nightmare of disillusion, the 'fall of the gods'. And when woman passes from the 'promise of rebirth' to construct in reality a path that is not maintained by a thousand enemies, when she refuses to be confused with images emanating from the other and begins the search for an identity which is her own, and not the image in the mirror, then other deceptions and impossibilities intervene in her relationship with herself.

What is reflected in a woman's desire is, therefore, confusion and loss of self, but also a pretext and defence against the difficulty of facing the unhappiness, limitations, and individual loneliness of her own body and her own destiny without laying the blame on other people. Man erects the bastion of the maternal-female dream against this same loneliness. All this is confirmed by the way that the figuration of women's cinema recaptures the early ideal forms that first embody women's desire.

The Androgyne, the Amazons, the mother goddesses of ancient times, are all figures that embody and signify omnipotence as opposed to power, as opposed to a desire that is subject to history. The figures belong to a dream produced by defeat but which is at the same time prophetic, that is characteristic of those who are both excluded from history but in advance of it. The dream opposes man's limited and defined sexuality with hermaphroditism and bi-sexuality and opposes the brutality of man's *real desires* with the authority of *ideal desires*.

Whereas man associates the Androgyne with nostalgia for the part of himself he projects on to the female, woman sees it as a dream encapsulating *rebirth* of a new Utopian individual unified under the sign of perfection. For women, therefore, attachment to infancy is both a defence and a trap within a history that cannot evolve because, before the issue can even find articulation, woman is anchored by the desperate need of the other, to a fixation perpetuating the misery, omnipotence, and unrestrained desire of infancy.

THE FEMALE LOOK

In classical cinema, the phantasmagoric image constructed by the cinematic apparatus converge with the narrative content (the love story) into a perfect combination, closing the circle just like a dream come true. In classical cinema the woman's look is denied, not only because the objectivizing, fetishistic look of a man or a voyeuristic boy is at the camera, but because her look has always been subsumed in his in the illusion of complementarity and completeness, in the same demand.

If cinema does construct a phantasm, the product of the male gaze focused on the female body, what remains unclear, for obvious reasons, is why woman should cling to that look: 'she feels at home in her illusion'.

The utter fascination with which the female spectator (though tragically disappointed in the last resort) responds to her own idealized image cannot, therefore, be shattered by a purely punitive attitude to cinematic pleasure, nor can it be related solely to the question of narrativity. The reasons are more profound, complex, and contradictory. If the woman spectator subsumes her desire into the man's, she can act out mimetically and hysterically her own active desire for the maternal body; she can also conserve, hiding behind the other's desire for possession, the dream of her infancy for *total fusion*.

Through primary identification with the camera, the 'excluded third party' becomes the *omnipotent controller* who can go on dreaming of being both father and mother, man and woman, participant and outsider.

In classical cinema, therefore, 'difference' is submerged into the possibility of *multiple identifications* whereby the woman is gradually allowed both the omnipotent look of primary identification (that of the pre-voyeuristic child) and the hysterical split look, both masculine and feminine, in which she sees herself as object of her own look, and assumes the power of the male look (as happens in hysteria according to Freud (1973: XVIII)).

In women's cinema, on the other hand, there is a kind of specularity. The first kind of look becomes more intense. As the female spectator's eyes meet those of the female director, the look is easier to isolate and to analyse. In women's cinema, where the camera reproduces the 'female look of the female spectator' in reality and in fantasy, the original significance of primary identification returns with tremendous force, almost, as it were, exaggerated or magnified.

The fantasy grows bigger before our eyes. To put it in dualistic terms, we could say that metonymy overwhelms metaphor and 'pictures' take precedence over narrative.

The scenes which the female spectator's look singles out, even in the narrative continuity of classical cinema (as can be seen in the videos by Adriana Monti, Giulia Alberti, and Paola Melchiori), are magnified in women's cinema as the gaze of the female spectator is duplicated and repeated by that of the female director.

The female spectator shows a preference for what could be called an 'ecstatic type' of look. Even in classical cinema, the woman spectator tends to single out 'scenes of fascination', treating them as pictures, pure and simple, immobile tableaux outside the narrative flow, though this effect can easily disappear if the narrative is particularly strong.

In women's cinema the fantasy develops in two different directions, that of deconstruction of the classical text and that of figuration of female identity.

The first direction is exemplified by Chantal Akerman's and Marguerite Duras's experimental use of film, in which the pleasure of looking at an object is replaced by the pure *pleasure of looking,* regardless of narrative. The absence of characters, the infinite expanse of the empty space (literally 'empty screen', *campo vuoto*; this implies a displacement of the human figure from the centre of the scene), the suspension of time, recall the experience of the child spectator, the third party, who is spellbound, paralysed, and trapped in an immobility produced by both 'intense involvement and terror' (Fachinelli 1983: Chapter X).

I like to think that in the deconstruction of the text, which is a vital part of experimental cinema, these women directors give a specific value to a model of *female fascination*: a hypnotic fascination (in the sense Freud gives in 'Group psychology and the formation of the ego'), a fascination with image, rather than with objects. This fascination, connected to the physical movement of the camera, is more significant than experimentation with language and indicates that a scene which was acted out in the distant past of each individual has been evoked.

This is another way of looking, which is closer to the sphere of ecstatic contemplation and mystical experience than to possession and the erotic. These points are reinforced by the form taken by the feminine in these women's films. Akerman's mother-daughter couple, Duras's double phallic body, Von Trotta's sister-mother couple convey a range of women's unconscious self-images.

Beneath what purports to be realistic use of imagery *extreme images* are hidden which are closer to a fantasy woman than to any real, specific woman. Akerman's figures disappear into the vastness of the empty space of the screen in answer to the mother's voice, as in *News from Home*; or they express (as in *Jeanne Dielman*) the overwhelming presence of maternal space, or the void of pure silence, as in *Toute une nuit*. Marguerite Duras's hieratic, idealized bodies in *India Song* frustrate phallic desire, craving as it does for inanimate perfection. In Von Trotta's films, the story of love between women, skilfully played on the threshold between sexuality, friendship, and family ties, highlights the split in the female unconscious between opposite polarities which inevitably reproduce the split between masculine and feminine. Von Trotta's 'sisters' oscillate between male and female, complementary and opposite, and mother and daughter locked in a life and death embrace. The girl friends in *Sheer Madness* show all the veracity and rigid artificiality that characterize the figures of the unconscious and primal phantasy.

In women's cinema the twofold problem which surrounds woman's self-imagery thus becomes clear: her self-image is caught between a fixation on infancy and figurations imposed by others. It is as if there were a double course to follow: escape from the total pervasiveness of male fantasy (which creates an illusion that signifies everything but is nothing) and then resistance to a specific identification (which is experienced paradoxically as a limitation rather than a liberation).

This of course relates to the impossibility of removing and/or overcoming the pivotal question of the Oedipus complex. That the resolution of the Oedipus complex is no solution for women is clear to all. What is less clear is that the unresolved Oedipus complex endures, accompanied by a search for female identity in the lasting absence of a given image.

Cinema as a place of fantasy, not far from the unconscious figurations that make free use of metaphor in writing and thought, highlights the present state of the problem: authentic figurations of the feminine – neither subordinate nor dominant – are proving slow to materialize. The internal obstacles include complicity with the male look and an 'absolute desire', a desire for servitude that conceals a desire for infancy, with all its misery and lack of constraint.

The discovery of a language, the awareness of a new symbolism, are crucial to how women and their condition can be represented. There is, as yet, no language of the feminine, any more than there is any image of autonomous female existence, only oscillation between the infantile and the fantastic, the execrable forms that the male libido has attributed to women and a defence against them.

Too often in cinema, the magic of the image as such combines with woman's desire to be seduced by her own omnipotent image. Her mirror reflects an image with no firm definition or clarity. Like an image reflected in water, it comes and goes. A slight ripple is enough to make it vanish.

NOTES

1 'Uroborus': mythical serpent, symbol of original perfection, the union of mother-child, male-female, etc.
2 See Fachinelli 1983, in particular chapters V and VI.

4 Conditions of illusion

GIULIA ALBERTI

Translated by Giovanna Ascelle

This paper results from work done in the '150 Hours' course, Women and Cinema, which was held in Milan from 1979 to 1983 and was developed as part of the teacher training element; that is, it was intended for women teaching the workers' evening classes initiated and organized by trade unions.

The issues raised were:

1 what representations of women are constructed by the cinematic language used in classical American and European films?
2 what kind of identification is offered to the female spectator?

At first the tool used to tackle these themes was textual analysis. For two years the students, together with two teachers, Adriana Monti and myself, studied cinema as a language, using textual analysis and analysing film sequences in still photographs. But after this phase, the course changed and became more like a research project, as our own and the students' interest moved from the film as text to the effects of this filmic text on the female spectator.

More specifically the new questions which arose were:

1 where does film position the female spectator?
2 what conditions induce cinematic pleasure and fascination in the female spectator?

3 what filmic construction produces fascination, the desire to look and be captivated by the screen images, that women feel at the cinema?

The questions were prompted by the kind of magnetic attraction that film held for us as women spectators. Watching and analysing the films, we noticed that the attraction was connected to particular scenes and images, and that the moments of high fascination were not due solely to the use of codes of cinematic language. We therefore resorted to another tool, psychoanalysis, and with its help we analysed the same scenes to find out what caused this attraction for us as women spectators.

The above questions show that our main interest was coming to focus on two issues: a) cinema as a form of representation which produces identities for women (what mechanisms produce this kind of effect in cinema as an institution?); b) woman as subject-spectator (what psychic mechanisms interrelate the woman spectator with cinema as an institution and enable cinema to condition female identity and create an imaginary to which she conforms?). The project therefore continued but with a new goal: we, as subject-spectators, had become the centre of the investigation, we, as spectators of a series of films, were the subjects and objects of analysis.

The next step was to find a form for the material derived from the analysis to enable us to explain this process of fascination to others. We did not want to use the written word but to do it cinematically. We consequently decided to make several short montage films, using images from the films we had studied but only those images which had held us fascinated. This resulted in eight films (on ¾-inch video), each about fifteen minutes long.

The films we worked on belonged to three different areas: a) classical American cinema (Hitchcock, Welles); b) films from the French *nouvelle vague* (Resnais, Godard); c) films by contemporary women film-makers (Duras, Akerman).

These were the premises and the procedures which gave rise to the film work presented here. Now I will try to analyse some of the ways in which the cinematic institution offers identification to women spectators. I would like to call these the 'conditions of illusion'.

Some further points should clarify my argument. This paper will deal with the development of a series of analyses I carried out on the 'subjective shot' in classical cinema (*Rebecca* and *Notorious* by Hitchcock) and in avant-garde films (like *News from Home* by Akerman). The analyses were published as articles in Italian magazines such as *Cinema e Cinema*, in the book *Sequenza segreta* and in the catalogue *L'immagine riflessa* (Alberti 1980, 1981, 1982). For this research I used textual analysis to establish the narrative position that had been given to the female character representing the 'look' in each film and to see how this affected the female spectator. Rather than analysing a single text, this paper first considers the different narrative structures and the different implications of the female characters' 'looks', and then considers how structural elements within one genre of film (the 'love story') are repeated with such effect that the same pleasure in looking is always induced in the female spectator.

In order to tackle the problem of identification I will first consider some distinctions between:

1 different categories of films: A) films directed by men; B) films directed by women;
2 different historical periods: a) classical films; b) avant-garde films;
3 the different elements in these films which induce fascination: in sections A) and a) the protagonist's body and the subjective shot; in sections B) and b) the empty space (see p.33) and the moving camera.
4 the different effects induced in the female spectator by the films in sections A), a) and B), b). I will call these effects 'fascination' and 'pleasure', respectively.

It is clear that the suggested distinctions are based not only on the director's sex but also on the cinematic strategies used in the films; these different strategies produce different effects, that is different kinds of attraction-participation in the female spectator.

My hypothesis is as follows: the conditions which create a state of fascination in the female spectator, the 'conditions of illusion', hinge on a psychic state which is emphasized, reproduced, and exploited by the cinematic strategies.

My first point of reference is the Freudian concept of subject identification defined as:

Psychological process whereby the subject assimilates an aspect, property or attribute of the other and is transformed, wholly or partially after the model the other provides. It is by means of a series of identifications that the personality is constituted and specified.   (Laplanche and Pontalis 1973)

Basically subject identification takes place in two ways: the ego can either be enriched or impoverished. I will deal with this concept in more detail later on.

In order to examine the mechanism of identification in film I will now look at the classical use of identification mechanisms, taking Hitchcock's use of them as an example.

The audience follows the sequence of actions in classical American cinema through the relation between the movement of the protagonist and the point of view of the camera. This can be done by the 'objective point of view' in which the character is

The following stills are from Alfred Hitchcock's *Rebecca* (1940), re-edited by Giulia Alberti, Adriana Monti and Paola Melchiori in their compilation videos

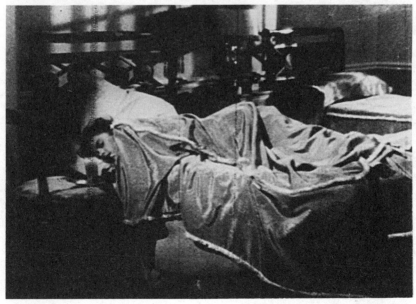

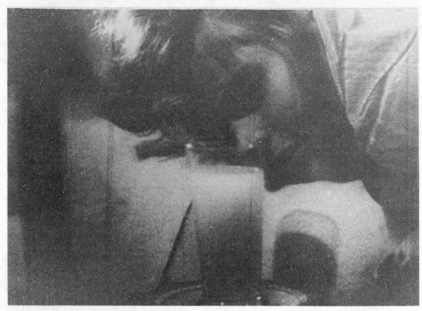

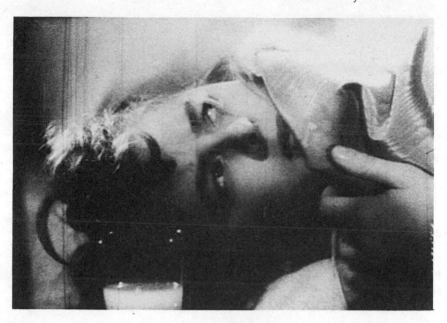

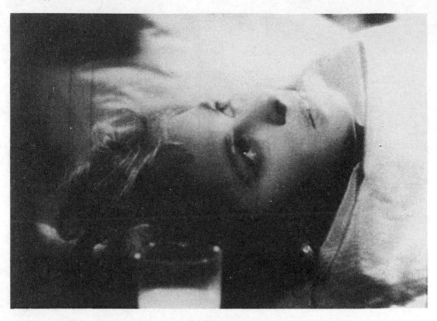

seen, as it were, from the outside and through the psychological mechanism of the ego ideal (a person seemingly better than oneself, on to whom one projects oneself) by which the spectator comes to project herself on to the screen character. The protagonist (the hero or heroine) is shown in an idealized form, without the contradictory elements belonging to reality. Alternatively, it can be done by the 'subjective point of view' shot, in which the female spectator literally assumes the position of the protagonist, so that there is no way of avoiding identification. The alternation between protagonist's point of view/seen object/protagonist's point of view makes the female spectator assume both the physical and the narrative position of the protagonist's state of mind so that she is forced to experience his or her narrative journey. The female spectator is able to watch the film and understand its narrative structure because she lets herself be put into someone else's place. The films to which I refer in this paper which use the subjective point of view are *Rebecca* and *Notorious*.

Let us therefore start by establishing the position that is given specifically to the female spectator in these two films. Through the mechanism of the subjective point of view, she is made to identify with the position of the protagonist. This is reinforced by sexual identity (the protagonist is female), by her narrative role (she is the heroine), by the protagonist's psychic state (a female figure who, though the protagonist, is not representative of adult womanhood).

Hitchcock chooses the cinematic strategy of the subjective point of view as an element structuring the whole narrative. This strategy makes the female spectator identify with the protagonist and temporarily abandon her own position (if she had it) of subject. In other words, the female spectator loses her distance from the protagonist, from the story, and from the film itself, loses her role as adult and mature subject.

Distance, otherness, and detachment characterize the psychic position of the adult subject, enabling him/her to judge, evaluate, and have a critical attitude towards life's events and, in this case, towards what is shown in a film. The female spectator, however, assumes a psychic position like that of a baby girl with her mother: she relives physical and psychic symbiosis with a female body, giving up her role of autonomous and self-determining subject in order to live as part of another body which secures her life. If she keeps this role of subjection and dependence (in other words of being totally dominated), she ensures her own survival. Even as an adult, a daughter might not break away from this relationship with her mother. Her way, then, of establishing relationships with reality, however distorted, of obtaining gratification, of living somehow, means living out the identification with the mother to the fullest extent, experiencing relationships and actions through the mediation of another person, her mother. This happens because the daughter cannot become a woman herself and does not dare to become an adult as she believes that only her mother can fulfil that role.

To continue with this parallel between the non-mature female subject and identification in the cinema, we will discuss the concept of identification in psychoanalytic terms.

Freud maintains that the subject can constitute itself either: a) by enriching the agency[1] of the psyche: 'the ego has enriched itself with the properties of the object, it has "introjected" the object into itself'; b) through the opposite process, where it is the object which 'replaces' the agency. The ego 'has surrendered' itself to the object: 'it has substituted the object for its own most important constituent' (Freud 1958: XVIII, 113).

In the case of the daughter-mother relationship, the former places the latter, a separate person, in the place of her ego ideal. This is the second of the two processes described above and implies an impoverishment of the personality. The subject does not enrich itself through assuming agencies which make it the subject of action, but renounces action by conferring on another being the right to act in its place.

From this analysis of the immature woman, we can see that the attitude of delegation inherent in her is similar to the role that the director requires the female spectator to play, calling on her to efface herself and let the film protagonist act in her place; only thus can she follow the film. The subjective point of view shot is the strategy that established female spectators in this kind of position and is perhaps so particularly effective (given the intense fascination which these films exert) because it plays on a psychic structure which is already present in many of them.

We can therefore say that the position which the 'subjective shot' creates for the female spectator recreates the psychic position which could exist between mother and daughter before the Oedipus complex has been resolved. To paraphrase the terms we used for identification in psychoanalysis, the protagonist-object 'is put in the place' of an agency of the female spectator's psyche. The protagonist takes the place of the female spectator's ego ideal. The subject chooses an ego ideal to conform to but instead of moving in person towards this ideal, it projects itself on to another subject which can act for it. As Freud says, the object is positioned in place of the ego ideal.

What causes this inability to act? The daughter's attitude is founded on her belief that a maternal prohibition stops her making a first-person choice of action. The original impetus for this kind of action would be the choice of a love object. The daughter would then have to define her own sexual identity as an autonomous subject separate from the mother figure. To be a woman who desires a man, to be adult, to have the same position as the mother, that of a woman with the right to have her own man: this is a primary action which makes all others possible. If the non-resolution of the Oedipus complex means that the woman does not regard herself as a female subject who can act, think, and love, this is because the maternal model is still her point of reference. Freud says that the super-ego of the daughter-subject gives the ego some rights and duties such as 'You should be like this' (meaning like the mother) but also tells it 'You have no right to be like that; many things are reserved for her.' This poses an insurmountable prohibition (see Freud 1958: XIX). Then, the only way for the subject to act without opposing this prohibition is to identify with another person who is doing what the subject would like to do, that is to identify with the actions of the mother or substitute figure who is doing what the subject cannot do without incurring maternal punishment.

This is where cinema comes in, latching on to woman's inability to fulfil her own desires, and offering an apt and sophisticated solution to this psychic need to delegate, since in film everything is anyway transposed into an imaginary world where all is permitted and there is nothing to interfere with subjects, prohibitions, or reality. Cinema gives the female spectator a role in which she can live the emotions and events that she is witnessing without having to be involved in a real sense.

This is how the enormous power to fascinate of the films we mentioned is set in motion, this is how the subjective point of view acquires its overwhelming strength. The subjective shot replaces the non-mature female spectator with a proxy, a film character enacts, on behalf of the subject, what it is not allowed to do for itself, that is, become a woman who desires a man, become a woman with the right to a man of her own.

If my analysis so far is accepted, it can be said that the 'subjective' technique's power of fascination is so strong and effective because it is based on an immature psychic structure in which action is delegated to a third person. Thus cinema as an institution fascinates by playing on psychic structures emanating from the unresolved Oedipus complex.

If, as we have seen, classical cinema derives a great deal of its power to fascinate from symbiosis between the female spectator and the protagonist, it encourages and stimulates the primary process of the psychic apparatus. According to Freud, this process is based on the reproduction of mnemic images of a hallucinatory nature on which a primary experience of satisfaction has conferred a privileged value.

Three consequences follow from this model of identification in cinema:

1 the female spectator finds a hallucinatory fulfilment through identifying with the character on the screen, and thus relives the experience of the child who looks and derives pleasure merely from looking;
2 the female spectator experiences the film as a hallucinated realization of her own desire, as an imaginary process; she thus avoids having to face real problems;
3 the female spectator, identifying herself fully with the screen character, cannot follow the development of the narrative from an objective, distanced position.

The distanced position is attached to the secondary psychic process. By exercising thought, attention, and judgement the female spectator achieves an adult position, is allowed to be herself and to follow the film from a position of otherness which stimulates a critical and creative attitude and puts her in a relationship with reality. Thus she is no longer merely searching for a repetition of primal pleasure, which keeps her tied to the realm of the imaginary. 'Thinking must concern itself with the connecting paths between ideas without being led astray by the intensity of those ideas' (Freud 1973: V, 602).

This position of otherness is found in Resnais's films, for example. He uses cinematic strategies to displace symbiotic identification and stimulate critical judgement (*Last Year at Marienbad* and *Providence*, for instance). In contrast to the classical films considered so far, the characters, as psychological and physical entities, are not the centre of attraction. Instead, their problems and relationships take on a central role. The female spectator is not called on to identify with the characters but to follow the problematics of the film as an adult subject, as herself.

Resnais does not try to bring about a symbiosis between the spectator and the protagonist; he tries to make the audience think, by using cinematic devices which prevent identification. The point of view used here is new and individual, neither objective nor subjective but cut off from the characters. It looks at them from a distance without being objective, because the composition chosen is predominantly 'anomalous or auteurish' in Jean Mitry's terminology (1965). But the most important element is the editing, the way images are split into narrative and visual fragments which are then drawn together. This creates constant breaks to which the spectator must respond by joining the pieces together. The point of view from which the film is told is not bound to the characters, but jumps from one place to another with no apparent connection. Continuity is dependent on a subtle logic which is defined by events and not by physical entities, and demands that the female spectator participates actively. She must draw on secondary psychic processes to summon the ability to follow the sequence of actions without letting her attention be distracted by those actions themselves or by the characters as such.

Thus, on the list of categories, the type of attraction experienced by the female spectator of Resnais's films should, I think, be called 'pleasure' rather than 'fascination'. 'Pleasure' includes the pleasure of thinking, organizing, following, and investigating, and drawing on one's intellectual skills as the subject concentrates on following what is happening, constructing and deconstructing narrative events. 'Fascination', on the other hand, connotes the magnetic power of attraction exerted by the image, by bodies and faces, which takes away the subject's willpower. The spectator then becomes a mere desiring subject overpowered by a passion to which it capitulates completely. The image captivates the female spectator and is designed principally to play on her emotions.

If Resnais's cinema indicates the possibility of a different type of identification, this means that cinematic strategies can be manipulated and used in different ways, and can stimulate the subject-spectator's various psychic abilities. These comments on Resnais's cinema can therefore lead us on to consider avant-garde strategies and the third type of identification. We should now discuss the kind of attraction produced by women directors working in the avant-garde.

In the first place, the strategies used in, and the related attraction produced by, *India Song* and *News from Home* are very different from those in the films so far considered.

The cinematic strategies which Chantal Akerman and Marguerite Duras use to guide the female spectator's attention seem to turn the usual strategies upside-down: there is no story to follow, no strong characters leading the narrative, no 'subjective' shots like those described above. Fascination is therefore produced neither by giving the look to the protagonist nor by the protagonist's body, as in classical cinema. In these women's films the body assumes a different value and is not, as in classical cinema, idealized. Here the female body is either entirely absent (*News from Home*) or so overwhelmingly present as to become obsessive (*India Song*).

In both films, the narrative reconstructs a psychic area and therefore comprises, not actions linked in a chronological development, but fragments of gestures, actions, and places ordered according to the logic of memory. In *India Song*, for instance, the recall of places, gestures, and tunes triggers the need to remember and brings the female spectator into touch with this area of the mind.

On a strictly cinematic level, the visual process that moves the female spectator is created by a particular use of point of view. On the one hand there is a totally immobile point of view which gazes at still or moving bodies or at empty spaces; on the other hand there are very slow deep-focus camera movements which show empty space or characters who seem more like hallucinations than human figures. Furthermore, the imposing body of a woman moves with difficulty in the frame, a mother's body which is more like a monument, a symbol, than a character in a story. The look of the camera dwells on this body with an ecstatic, captivated gaze which cannot be detached from the scene which is unfolding.

The elements I have just described indicate a strategy which makes identification with the character in the frame impossible;

and indeed there is no character who looks in spite of the camera's attentive gaze. The camera makes a very precise observation of each scene as it develops and accurately describes the relationship between its look (the look of the woman behind the camera) and the woman in the frame. What does the camera's look say? And what in this look fascinates the female spectator?

The ecstatic fascination overwhelming the female subject who guides the camera's look recalls the look of a daughter captivated by her mother's image: the daughter looks at the mother and admits her pleasure in looking at her, but at the same time this representation blocks any possibility of action. The daughter can contemplate the maternal body to her heart's content, as it moves in this rarefied universe. But this mother exists only as a symbol, not as a character to whom action is delegated as in classical cinema. She does not act and the film does not develop around action.

What *India Song* constructs and displays is the simultaneous presence of a body on show and a gazing eye: the eye is external to the film; you cannot see it but it is there, providing the motivation for that spectacle, the presence of that body. But the spectacle conveys nothing but immobility, the look is fascinated and petrified. The daughter cannot act.

If classical cinema used the unresolved Oedipus complex to arouse and sustain fascination, then women's cinema makes this point, this difficulty, explicit, with its obsessive representation of the power of the maternal body before which the daughter must give way. In this case fascination rather than pleasure is certainly the means by which the film-maker attracts the spectator. But wherever the look is emphasized it is as a function and not through a physical presence. It does not belong to a character who then, inevitably, becomes the spectator's proxy, acting in her place: here, on the contrary, the look is shown as a psychic attitude and as such is presented through the spectacle on the screen. But this use of fascination, even if intended as a way of indicating the quality of the look, attracts the spectator into a vortex of inaction and deprives her of any critical judgement.

In *News from Home* the cinematic elements already described are taken to extremes: the static point of view, the absence of narrative, the empty spaces that recur throughout the entire film, all produce fascination and pleasure and all draw attention to the absence of a body, so allowing for it to be represented in phantasized form, and thus vaster and more powerful. It is the empty space that makes use of absence to represent the phantasized presence of the mother. But the pattern formed by the empty spaces, consisting of streets and places in New York, enable the female spectator to be an active participant. She is called on to collaborate in the film by establishing connections and following the rhythms and alternations of the shots. If her secondary process and her intellectual and critical skills fail to engage, she is cut off from the film and will experience neither pleasure nor fascination. The engagement she must make is connected to the look, to identification with the camera in its seeing capacity, and not to a (non-existent) protagonist as a psychological entity she can attach herself to.

The difference between the identification strategies in *News from Home* and in classical cinema lies in the fact that in the former the female spectator identifies with the camera itself. No one else acts for her, because there is no action and the only active element is the look of the camera and the look of the female spectator. She takes on the role of observer as she cannot identify with a body (as none is there), nor can she act through another woman (as none is there). Thus the female spectator is made to identify solely with herself, with the seeing function, with the very position of spectator, because she can take no action. The action which is usually carried out by the image of an adult woman on the screen cannot be performed. And the daughter's position of immaturity is presented through an interplay between fascination, pleasure, and dismay.

Classical cinema presents a kind of hallucinatory satisfaction of desire which gives the female spectator an immature role in that this hallucinated pleasure is always repeated and always lets her act through proxy. In Duras's and Akerman's films that type of satisfaction becomes impossible. Instead emphasis is given to what constitutes the crucial problem for women in the construction of their identity as autonomous and mature adults. These films make it impossible for the female spectator to delegate action to the protagonist, to construct a proxy to act in her place. These films expose the structure of delegation, reveal the impasse lived by the female spectator, and indirectly press for a way out of this inaction.

What emerges clearly in these two films is the structure of the

immature woman's psyche: she cannot make an active confrontation with life or the object of love. They show the female spectator where the root of the problem lies, so that it cannot be
avoided. A series of new strategies gives the female spectator a
different role from that allocated to her by classical cinema and in
this new role she is made to live out non-action, she is transformed into a mere seeing function while, at the same time, being
made aware of the process.

The female spectator no longer submits to taking action
through displacement into someone else's body. Instead she is
taken back to the centre of the problem which gave rise to her
inability to define and acquire an identity. She can analyse her
condition and can go back to square one in terms of representation and identity. She can observe and confront the 'conditions
of illusion'. Can the new cinema help expose the 'conditions of
illusion' and enable the female spectator to become reunited with
herself and achieve the construction of her own identity?

NOTE

1 agency (*istanza*):

> Freud's different expositions of the psychical apparatus generally
> used the terms 'system' or 'agency' to designate the parts or sub-
> structures of this apparatus. Although the two terms are often
> used interchangeably, it is worth noting that while 'system'
> refers to a more exclusively topographical approach, 'agency' has
> both the topographical and a dynamic meaning.
>
> (Laplanche and Pontalis 1973)

5 Ecstasy, coldness, and the sadness which is freedom

LEA MELANDRI

Translated by Kate Soper

MODESTY AND SHAMELESSNESS

We are inclined to think of modesty in primarily sexual or moral terms. But there is a tradition of common sense that associates it particularly with a retreat into 'private' or 'emotional' life. Modesty is the 'veil' with which one protects a *dream of erotic felicity* whose excesses would prove too shameful were they to be experienced publicly – excesses of joy and pain, the deathly chill of separation, ecstatic reunions in which two people seem to fuse into one.

This dream of love has nevertheless been given some currency in the form of a more overt *shamelessness*, even if its channels of diffusion have been rather limited – being confined, for example, to the quasi-anonymity of lonelyhearts columns or radio phone-ins, to the cultural undergrowth of romantic fiction, the photo-romance, and pop music – those impoverished descendants of melodrama and operatic lyrics – and above all, to movies and television dramas about love, an archive of illusions, where the images and events of 'private life' can be displayed to a million eyes without losing their aura of privacy.

There is a deep-rooted predilection for this dream of love, most notably and dramatically on the part of women, and the dream

profoundly *resists* critical investigation. This is clearly evidenced
in the fact that a particular kind of material (either written or
visual) is instantly recognizable to everyone and holds its audience spellbound with a magic, self-contained totality, wholly
remote and separate from any actual experience. It is also shown
by the fact that any critical analysis of this material is almost inevitably bound to take place at a different moment in time (the
dream must take place at a different time from the one in which it
is assessed), and this must be carried out by a different person
(the dreamer can seldom be persuaded to write an account of the
object of his or her dream). So thus it is that the dream always
preserves its *grandiose* quality, and critical thought preserves
stainless modesty.

Looking for an account of these aspects of 'private life' that is
not wholly divorced from common sense, we must look to the
writings of some authors who, although not particularly well
known, have their own special importance precisely because
they have illuminated facets of our lives upon which mainstream
culture is usually silent. In the words of Paolo Mantegazza, the
naturalist and anthropologist (who lived at the turn of the
century):

> Love, from the moment of its initial and most confused appear-
> ance, is choice; it is a deep and irresistible sympathy between
> different natures, it is the resolution of component forces, the
> harmonization of opposites, the bringing together of what is
> disjointed; it is the harmony of harmonies.
> (Mantegazza 1879: 71)

This image of masculine desire presents the dream of love as
essentially nostalgic for an imaginary happiness, in which oppo-
sites would be recomposed and harmony prevail among pre-
viously discordant parts. Thanks to the profound and irresistible
attraction between a man and a woman, all the divisions and
oppositions of the social order will, supposedly, be reunited: the
divisions of mind and body, of strength and docility, of male and
female, in short the poles of a *duality*, which for all its abstract and
imaginary quality continues to exert a significant influence both
on the lives of individuals and on the history of our civilization in
general.

Viewed from the perspective of this ideal of an almost divine
harmony, a sense of modesty can be seen as a kind of threshold

between the earthly and the heavenly, between time and eternity: it is the *veil* of 'privacy' and 'intimacy', the guardian of that 'perfect being', which, although it figures only in a dream, is 'the sum of man and woman'. As Max Scheler wrote:

> The sense of modesty is therefore rooted in a kind of disequilibrium, in a certain *disharmony* between the meaning and demands of the spiritual life, on the one hand, and its bodily requirements, on the other. . . . It is a feeling, in consequence, in which we can detect a strange and enigmatic association of the 'spiritual' and the 'carnal', of the 'infinite' and the 'finite', of 'essence' and 'existence'.
>
> (Scheler 1979: 21)

This idea of a perfect and infinite happiness, protected by nostalgia and hope, and presiding over both the past and the future, expresses the *religion* which masculine desire has conjured up in order to hold together what has been separated in actual life: it is the dream of children, who realize, as they grow older, that they cannot always have their mother with them. No ordinary dwelling place can accommodate such a singular unity as this dream of love, a unity which is simultaneously human and divine. What is needed for a 'perfect being', a fusion of two organisms into one, is a church – and what man has found as a protective enclave for his dream, a temple of privacy and security, is the home, and within the home, the body of the woman.

> Two organisms, but a single sense; two worlds in their externality, yet united by a common centre; two nerves whose different paths impel a difference of sensation, yet intertwine and run in parallel around a single heart. . . . Two solitary barques in the empty space of the ocean plough the waves, each unaware of the other: a quiver of sympathy runs through their sails and rigging and causes them to creak in unison: they feel themselves constrained by a common exigence and throw out a life-line to each other. Henceforth, they will cleave their way through the same waters, be exposed to the same dangers, sigh together in their eagerness for land.
>
> (Mantegazza 1879: 98)

Infinite as the 'empty space of the ocean', yet as rigorously secret as a hallowed sanctuary, the woman's body becomes the ideal terrain for an encounter which must be solitary and removed from prying eyes. But for that same reason, it loses its real contours and its full sexual individuality and acquires instead the dimensions of the purely maternal – becoming a hollowed space, empty and capacious, a vessel destined to accommodate a son.

Modesty, at this point, becomes a dowry, a property peculiar to women, who in their role as priestesses of the temple must guard against all possible violations by the male, whose veneration for the sanctuary does not rule out aggressive impulses. This delicate veil of modesty or virginity, behind which the man shelters his childish dream, is also the barrier of resistance to his guerrilla assaults.

> Virginity is the sacred veil which falls across the entrance to the temple wherein men are born. Tear this most fragile of veils, and though you be youthful, though you be beautiful, though you be no less pure than the day before, you are no longer in the realm of the divine. The temple has been violated, the idol shattered. . . . Open temples are always less sacred than closed ones.   (Mantegazza 1879: 122, 125)

The penetrated body loses its holiness and like a territory vanquished in war must humbly offer itself in obedience.

> She has already yielded up her heart and all her affection to her god; today she hands over the seal which guarantees his possession of everything she owns . . . naked, weak, unarmed, she entrusts herself to a powerful, armed, invulnerable man. . . . An angel only yesterday, today she lets her lover strip her of her wings, that she may become a woman, a wife, a friend, a mother. Priestess of the temple, she burns her white vestal robes upon the altar of love, and pronounces with sobbing cries of joy and grief: 'I am yours, I am all yours . . . I have clipped my wings that I may be borne aloft on your genius; I have forgone my own religious aspirations in order to become, quite simply, your companion; do not betray me. . . . May your love for me be as vast as my own humbleness towards you.'
>   (Mantegazza 1879: 125–6)

The liberated woman of modern society is tolerated, but not as our equal; she is marked for life, like the orphan who lives within a family to which he never properly belongs. Should a woman pass from being a mistress to being a mother, a great space still divides her from becoming a true woman, or to put it

better, a man-woman, a veritably noble creature, who thinks
and feels as a woman and thus lends completeness to my own
universe. (Mantegazza 1879: 149)

Woman enters history under the sign of *mutilation* and *death*.
Under cover of love, a subterranean war is waged whose effects
are profoundly destructive. Once she has forfeited her 'white
vestal robes', the woman must don the garb of the *slave* and the
orphan; once she has given birth to life, she must beg for her sub-
sistence; once having fancied herself divine, she must now do
what she can to be like a man.

The original unity, which continues to be envisaged in terms of
harmony and happiness, and whose illusion is reborn in every
encounter of love, gives way to the 'divided' and 'disjointed'
forces referred to by Mantegazza. But these 'different natures'
(masculine and feminine, mind and body, interiority and the
outer world, fullness and emptiness, life and death, etc.) are in
reality *contrary pairs* which, on coming together, react according
to a pre-existing complementarity.

That which a real *diversity* would have simply made possible,
becomes a matter of fate and necessity: the *site of lack* is fated to
become a site of expectation and promise; similarly, emptiness
aspires to be filled, that what is opaque seeks the clarity of understanding, the orphan craves kinship, the woman yearns for a man
or the son in whom she may find her own fullness and wholeness.

More realistically – though again the image is not without its
mythical significance – Freud compares modesty to pubic hair,
and this in turn to the art of weaving:

> Shame, which is considered to be a feminine characteristic *par
> excellence*, but is far more a matter of convention than might be
> supposed, has as its purpose, we believe, concealment of geni-
> tal deficiency. We are not forgetting that at a later time shame
> takes on other functions. It seems that women have made few
> contributions to the discoveries and inventions in the history
> of civilisation; there is, however, one technique which they
> may have invented – that of plaiting and weaving. If that is so,
> we should be tempted to guess the unconscious motive for the
> achievement. Nature itself would seem to have given the
> model which this achievement imitates by causing the growth
> at maturity of the pubic hair that conceals the genitals.
> (Freud 1964: 132)

Virginity, or pubic hair, like Penelope's weaving, functions as a sign of what is lacking or lost, while serving to create the illusion of its presence. According to Freud's definition, modesty can thus be thought of as a veil allowing concealment of two different and apparently antithetical conditions: a state of misery, emptiness, and mutilation on the one hand, a dream of wholeness and contented repleteness on the other.

Coming back to the very widespread tendency to identify modesty with shame, one might, in the light of this, suggest that people feel as ashamed of their grief as of their happiness – or rather, that they are at a less conscious level ashamed of the particular and contradictory bond which unites, as two faces of the same coin, the emotions of grief and joy, the ideas of life and death, of sacrifice and reward, weakness and strength, etc. 'Private life', in short, seems to act in accordance with an economy of survival peculiarly its own: an economy wherein are reconciled, however illusorily, modes and conditions which in the order of society and culture at large are regarded as *dualistic*, divided, and incompatible.

There are some clear examples one might cite here: just as women have had to acknowledge that despite their very evident situation of oppression and subordination, the spirit of rebellion does not come easily to them, so they have had to recognize that the sense of feminine 'wholeness', for all the superior strength, freedom, and intelligence that go into its making, does not necessarily coincide with genuine self-fulfilment and the acquisition of real autonomy.

If the man's dream of love as reuniting what has been violently severed (childhood and history, mother and son, strength and tenderness, etc.) strikes us as surprising, it is even more paradoxical that in the experience of so many, if not all, women, life and death, domination and submission, joy and sorrow, everything and nothing, etc., should inevitably combine together.

From the man's point of view, as revealed in Mantegazza's account, it is a case of achieving a harmony of 'different' and 'complementary' natures (of reconciling the 'active' with the 'affective', the 'public' with the 'private', or, as Max Scheler puts it, 'spiritual demands' with 'bodily requirements'). The components of this supposedly happy and fulfilled state of original unity are depicted in very similar fashion in the woman's 'dream'. The Platonic myth of the Androgyne, and the Christian story of Adam and Eve appear in almost identical form in both the masculine and feminine versions of the dream. As Virginia Woolf puts it:

> One has a profound, if irrational instinct in favour of the theory that the union of man and woman makes for the greatest satisfaction, the most complete happiness. . . . Coleridge perhaps meant this when he said that a great mind is androgynous. It is when this fusion takes place that the mind is fully fertilised and uses all its faculties. . . .
>
> Some collaboration has to take place in the mind between the woman and the man before the act of creation can be accomplished. Some marriage of opposites has to be consummated.
>
> (Woolf 1929: 147–8, 157)

But if we look at the manner in which women have sought unconsciously to exploit and profit from this male-imposed duality (male-imposed in the sense that it both grounds male sentiment and shapes a patriarchal civilization), then we discover significant differences. For men, the dream represents a prolongation of childhood, which continues alongside and in parallel with their social history, thus allowing them to be child and adult simultaneously, and to impose an order and a division of labour compatible with the control and unification of the different sides of their life. Women, on the other hand, in the interests of preserving a *right to childhood* and of giving themselves an appearance of autonomy, have sought – through an imaginative project that combines something of both mysticism and omnipotence – to blend or conflate the different elements of the dream. Thus they aspire to be both mother and child, fullness and emptiness, absolute abundance and absolute loss, warmth and frigidity, richness and penury, the origin of life and its absence.

What is, for the one sex, merely a dream of loving happiness, figures for the other as a *struggle for self-creation* – as the quest for a specifically feminine 'rule' or 'order' which is sometimes viewed as something to be opposed to the order of masculine culture, at other times as that which would humanize it and temper its violence. On the other hand, as Sibilla Aleramo has written, if women had not been so 'hasty and fearful' in displaying their dreams, with their whole burden of both grief and exaltation, they would have seen more clearly that it is precisely the hopes, the expectations and the pretences, the illusions and the delusions, sustained by the dream, which present the major obstacle and strongest resistance to the realization of any real and authentic autonomy.

The link with childhood which is maintained in the dream allows the woman to see herself as orphaned and needing love and thus as having a claim on the maternal warmth she never enjoyed in reality. In this capacity, it is an attempt, though a purely illusory one, to guarantee the woman's birth and existence. But it also acts as a block to the realization of her genuine potential for autonomy.

In the writings of Sibilla Aleramo (1878–1960), which represent perhaps the most exhaustive attempt by a woman to give voice to all the thoughts which the modesty of our culture seeks to suppress, we find combined together an expression of the dream's rapture, a luminous analysis of it from a feminine point of view, and a charting of the route by which a woman, almost in spite of herself and unconsciously, comes into possession, from somewhere beyond the long sleep of childhood, of a freedom which is all the more desirable because of its remoteness, whose actual enjoyment is a 'sadness' and source of regret. That this richest of autobiographical testimonies still awaits 'discovery' even within the more educated circle of women (Aleramo was herself aware of being ahead of her times) is explicable only if we remember that the intimacy of the dream is such that even when it overcomes the first barrier of modesty and reveals itself, it none the less ultimately constitutes, in its turn, a kind of veil, whose effect is to screen from view a reality whose presentiment is too painful. Aleramo herself says that we do not know whether the greater pain lies in sleep or in life.

It is only unbeknown to herself, and one might almost say despite herself, given the note of unhappiness with which she speaks in her *Diari* of the 'necessity of living for oneself', that Aleramo comes to discover the genuine autonomy of the feminine being. It is therefore hardly surprising if her readers have overlooked this less grandiose and more disquieting journey towards a freedom which is the 'liberating' but at the same time the 'melancholy' consequence of renouncing one's childhood dream.

THE DREAM'S TWOFOLD QUALITY: COLDNESS AND ECSTASY

I shall proceed in two stages, first concentrating on the nature of the dream of love which suffuses the life of writers like Aleramo, and then turning to what is most original and advanced in her account: her quest for that freedom which, as she puts it in her *Diari*, is also a 'sadness'.

Between the relationship with her son, described in her novel *A Woman* (1979b), and the affair with Franco Matacotta (recorded in her diary as *un amore insolito*), between the first and the 'ultimate illusion', there intervened a 'terrifying confusion' of other loves which are documented both in her private writings (her letters) and in her publications (novels, poetry), and through which Aleramo gradually comes to realize that all different forms of love are governed by much the same law: the alternation between life and death, illusion and disappointment.

At the same time, in her frequent comparisons of male and female responses, Sibilla sheds light on the individual moves and different rationalities coexisting within a dream which, in all essentials, remains common to both men and women. From the time of the birth of her son and her life with Giovanni Cena, which Aleramo describes as 'something more serious than a marriage', it is apparent that the *law of survival*, which lies at the basis of the ideal unity of love, is quite different for one who has incorporated his dream into the fabric of social reality, from what it is for one who continues, as the woman does, to trust to the dream to realize her own birth and entry into history.

As she puts it in *A Woman*:

> Gradually I became aware of my maternal feelings. At last I had a reason for living, an obvious duty. . . .
> For a week I lived in a magnificent dream. I had boundless emotional energy which warded off exhaustion and allowed me to think that I was beginning to take control of my life.
> (Aleramo 1979b: 45–6, 50)

Sibilla associates her pregnancy with her emergence from under the 'black cloud' of a year of unhappy marriage. She was able to regard the new growth within her body as destined to regenerate integral parts of herself. To it she would transmit her 'blood', her 'youth', and all her 'dreams' but in the transfigured sublimity of 'perfect beauty', 'perfect health', 'absolute greatness'.

This conflation of herself with her child enables her to forget the feeling of being orphaned which she had always experienced in her relationship with her mother: in her illusion, the life growing within her is magnified, takes on such dimensions as to encompass the maternal embrace of which she herself was deprived, it encircles her and is encircled, both gives and receives warmth, in a seeming fusion of mother and child.

At other times, this perfect coexistence of two persons within one is shown in a more disquieting light: it figures as dominion, as tyrannical reciprocity, and mutual engulfment: 'he is my son, and, being my son, he will be like me. I want to take him, hold him, absorb him completely so that after a time I would disappear and he would become entirely *me*' (Aleramo 1979b: 175).

> That ferocious greed for annihilation, that instant of consciousness – who is to say whether it is less or more than human? – in which the woman rebels against nature, rebels at being at the service of life; and then that transition from hate to love, that docile acceptance, that rapture, and, finally, that unique but fearsome compensation – that absolute feeling for all eternity, that the child is hers, only hers.   (Schnitzler 1929: 11)

In any case, the aspiration to give birth to herself through the medium of her child and to draw life from its young life, is revealed as illusory: the potent, intelligent, feminine individuality which Sibilla is awaiting does not materialize.

A woman who has just given birth undergoes a sort of mystical transfiguration. She becomes superhuman, possessed of the 'happiness of an atom within the Infinite'. Present time, imbued with a 'radiant mystery', merges with eternity. In place of a 'pathetic creature imploring pity', there arises a divinity.

But following swiftly upon this 'resurrection' comes a feeling of dying, the sensation that all one's own energies have been transfused to the other.

> In fact apart from the energy I expended on the child I was increasingly unable to look around me, to want anything or to do anything: it was as if mental weariness had been superimposed on physical exhaustion. I was dissatisfied with myself, reproached myself with having neglected my best qualities . . . . The mother and the woman in me couldn't live together.   (Aleramo 1979b: 53)

In the dream of love, abundance and vacuity, control and loss of self, are mutually entwined, and constantly vying for position in a contest whose effect is to undermine any attempt on the woman's part to channel her energies into the creation of an authentic being. Poised like a mountain over an abyss, the harmony that had seemingly been retrieved can only collapse and wait to re-emerge.

A relationship with a man, tested over a long period of cohabitation, like that of Aleramo and Cena, has a rather similar result:

Just now I was watching *him* writing: he cannot give me what I lack. But I can give to him, who has genius, the quiet peace which allows him never to lose his way in life. I must stand by his side, I have a reason to exist, even if as an individual I am incapable of handing on any thought or feeling.

(Conti 1978: 170)

And shortly I weep, I weep in the weakness of my womanly being, of a being undermined by original sin. . . . Here are *his* works: his latest volume, in which there is something of me, which he could not have written without my love . . . he has gone back to life, to action . . . as a human being I ought to take pride in that, but I don't, I act like a child, I cry. Why? Thus I lean, every so often, over the abyss, in order for the horror of it to drag me back, in order to hear my son's voice in the distance imploring my salvation.

(Aleramo 1932: 97)

But beyond the veil which holds her in thrall to the two poles of an imaginary duality (mind–body, life–death, tenderness–strength, etc.), and commits her to a futile struggle for unity across this divide, Sibilla begins to see more clearly how male culture has inscribed its limits at precisely those points where she feels the most insistent urge to trespass. These 'natural differences' (masculine–feminine, mind–body, nature–history, etc.) are neither founded in a harmonious totality, nor provide any basis from which to return to it. On the contrary, they are the products of a masculine law in accordance with which the role and function of every person have already been predetermined.

Ineffable metamorphosis of love in tenderness, the immeasurable step from freedom to servitude, the obscuring of desire, the ticking of the clock, the regular ticking of the clock.

(Aleramo 1932: 97)

Man relates to me as if, by comparison, I were something inanimate: as if I were a flower, a nest, a star: and in no sense whatsoever am I an accomplice of his secret labours – neither in his bold assault upon reason and form, nor in his conceptualization, nor in his architecture: I am woman, presented under the guise of eternity, immobile, contemplative, remote.

(Aleramo 1932: 95)

You have no need of my spirit – I said to him, watching him while he slept – and why should you notice that it suffers? You have your own to nourish, to conserve, to defend. You believe us one, and we are two. It is you who stands at the centre of the world, you with your unchanging outlook upon the world, your mental stronghold. What did you lack, you poor, overgrown baby? Only a sense of physical equilibrium – which I was there to provide. At night, lying with your hand across my breast, you have all that you need in its comforting beat. Such is your love, a love which knows neither the raging thirst for devotion, nor the voluptuousness of excess. There is nothing in you of that dizziness which comes over me, of that preparedness to dissolve myself, if you should wish it, if I have to, if your mission in life, your own best interests, demand it. This luminous drowning of my being . . . this desire to be absorbed in everything, this weariness with everything.

(Aleramo 1932: 115)

In this splitting of 'spirit' and 'nature', of childhood and history, of masculine and feminine, man has constrained woman to become a silent spectator, an atmosphere caressing his thoughts, a body bringing him relief from his labours at the end of the day, a place where the 'baby' within him can always be guaranteed maternal comfort.

For Sibilla, who persistently tried to rouse herself from this 'mood of exhaustion' with its 'doleful lament', to decipher its 'asthmatic logic', and to throw off the 'leaden chains' of its abstract nomenclature, all that remained were the unhappy privileges of motherhood: the striving to promote the happiness of others in default of her own, the capacity to appreciate 'the goodness of life' though always aware that her own power to achieve it was subjugated, aware of the sense of the fullness of everything in its very impoverishment.

Confronted with the man's obvious centrality, his need for 'physical equilibrium' gratified in the possession of the female body, the image of an ideal unity collapses: we are not one, says Sibilla, but two, one (male) at the centre, the other (female) at the periphery and eager at once to break the bounds to be dispersed within the terrain of the one, both to overwhelm him with her own omniscience and to dissolve herself within him that he may discover himself.

During the years in which Aleramo, through her involvement in mass education projects and feminism, engaged in the construction of an image of a potent and all-conquering motherhood – an image of a 'virginal maternity', through whose realiza tion 'modern ascetic womanhood' would rouse humanity from its torpor – she made brief notes and comments of extraordinary lucidity, simply out of 'the need for self-knowledge':

> The modern woman's most persistent feeling *vis-à-vis* her own survival: an outward sense of gentility, implying weakness and servility, deep impulses towards devotion, a readiness to give herself over to the beloved and to the pursuit of his happiness without any comparable joy to herself (1908). . . .
>
> You men are strong because everything comes easily to you, because nothing wastes your energy, because your forces are indefinitely conserved. . . . I who have struggled to give voice to my silent commentary, who have yearned to shoulder loads beyond the weight of my own body . . . I am weak because the whole of this long monstrous labour serves only to place me at your mercy, at the mercy of you . . . who have no knowledge of the effort of self-regeneration, of carrying on after you have been struck down. . . .
>
> An inner sense of contempt for herself, an exaggerated estimation for her oppressors, love and hate combined.
>
> (Aleramo 1978b: 176, 178, 181)

In these notes, and in remarks in *Lettere d'amore a Lina* (Aleramo 1982b), written during the same period, we find Aleramo breaking free of the magical and mystical dream of complementarity and interchangeability between the contraries of life and death, joy and grief. The Woman's disappearance from history, her self-abnegation in devotion to man, are no longer viewed as allowing access to a fuller life, but for what they are in reality: self-contempt, exaggerated esteem of the other. The dream of fullness, harmony, and union is revealed as the man's dream, as a fantasy which only benefits him. For the woman, who had thought to find her own existence through the medium of his, the dream figures as an 'instinct to tyrannize', as 'enslavement'.

I have always felt myself to be the only reality in a world of amorphous forms. . . . But behold, this me, with my instinct for love, for beauty, for harmony, is infinitely cruel, and insists on insane sacrifices . . . I am the slave of my own instinct for grandeur. (Aleramo 1982b: 59)

Only through her encounter with Lina, brief though it was, did Aleramo sense the truth of her own being, and reach out to a self as yet unborn who would be freed of 'myth' and illusion. 'I am born in this moment and for this moment alone . . . this birth will come to me like a blinding revelation, as a truth of incomparable radiance in which all the myths of my previous existence are transcended' (Aleramo 1982b: 32).

Her correspondence with Umberto Boccioni and Dino Campana reveals further insights into fundamental structures of thought that are concealed by the dream of wholeness and absoluteness in love. The letters to Boccioni make it clear that the woman's devotion is also an expression of her desire for control; that the impulse to 'mould' others is part of her quest for her own form, in other words that it speaks of a *struggle for self-creation*. What comes to the fore in the letters to Campana, and is revealed with increasing clarity, is the woman's *disposition to assume the role of the child*: her illusion of confirming in the man his own need for tenderness and maternal warmth.

Encountering in Boccioni the typical 'strong' man, resistant to the snares of love, and not to be seduced by the charms of a mere difference of sexuality, Sibilla finds herself forced to cast off her own strong image in order to expose her inner frustration and need for love, and to give voice to the 'baby' within her which 'craves the new-born infant's bliss'.

You have spent a lot, too much, of your time in communicating strength and courage to others less able than yourself, to people suffering from inner corruption and outward indecision. You are trapped in a process of introspection, in a consuming analysis which seeks to communicate the incommunicable; which seeks to divide that which has to remain indivisible, personal, and individual to the bitter end. You thought that in the fusion with a woman you would create a unity. . . . Nothing could be more mistaken. What we need is a grand conception, some project for which we work unilaterally. Even as I write, I am put in mind of the thousand problems of the inner life, its

anguish, its possibilities, its fusions, affinities, passions, sacrifices. . . . I throw all that out of the window with disgust.
(Conti and Morino 1981: 88)

No one has ever seen me sleep. I myself have kept watch over
so many sleeps. How many lives have I drawn breath for! Do
you know that you are the only strong man I have ever met? I
had to mould myself under the illusion that I was shaping
others. I had to persist, as you say in your letter, in this construction upon shifting sands – in this discovery of my essential self.
(Conti and Morino 1981: 102)

I so long for joy! I reach out for it like a new-born baby. In these
last weeks, I have got to grips with life, because I have been
hoping to be back with you. What's the point of pride? Why
lie? One cannot live without love. I love you. I need you.
(Conti and Morino 1981: 101)

The story of the love-affair with Dino Campana has all the
drama of a childhood nightmare, all the tenderness of a dream.
On account of experiences – madness and subsequent recovery
in a mental asylum – which Campana happened to share with
Sibilla's own mother, the relationship is subject to a curious
reversal, whereby Sibilla claims protection and maternal attention from a man whom she regards as a 'child', a 'savage', and a
'madman'.

Sibilla sends a photograph of herself as a child to him, and rests
in his arms like an 'exhausted baby'. No sooner does the poet
seem 'tall', 'strong', and 'lucid', than she loses her stature, and
becomes, in comparison, a 'poor, inglorious little creature'. Her
mother's memory was to impinge later in a more directly autobiographical manner at the point of final separation, following
Campana's recovery in the Castel Pulci asylum.

In this affair, too, it is the notion of being *orphaned* which predominates: the fate of the madman is to be envied in that he at
least has someone to attend him. What emerges, however, more
clearly than in her other relationships is the self-directed aspect
of her desire to 'cure' the man. In her eagerness to nourish him
and restore him to vigour, we can detect her own longing for her
mother to throw off her weakness and become a strong, protective companion to her; for Campana to be transformed from a
helpless child into a self-confident adult, and thus in a position to

offer her parental care; for him to stop being mad and allow her to become so herself.

This exalted image of herself as ministering angel and redeemer serves as a grandiose façade concealing her inner vulnerability: on its collapse what is revealed is her deep urge to acknowledge her infantile needs for what they are, without having to inflate them into something more sublime or to erect them into either cross or altar.

The dream of love is the expression not only of the woman's desire for birth and self-creation, but also the *imaginary place* in which the right to a childhood which she had never really had is finally recognized, as also is the expectation that she will be compensated for never having known maternal love or filial contentment.

In her later love-affairs, this grandiose but double-edged dream, in which life and death are equally exalted, loses its heroic dimensions and becomes fragmented. Abandonment is no longer experienced as an urge to immediate fulfilment. Instead, it is the emptiness it reveals which becomes the object of scrutiny and investigation, and which is now recognized as a need for love, as fragility, as emotional impoverishment.

Where once *ecstasy* and *coldness* had been treated as two confused aspects of the same experience, they are now perceived as distinct, and separate in time; this allows insight into what is innate and excessive in their character.

In the epistolary novel, *Amo dunque sono* (Aleramo 1982a), the love relation develops in a context of imposed separation: the letters are addressed to a real person, but cannot be dispatched on account of a mutual agreement. To add to the pain of separation and the yearning for reunion, there is the gap in age between Sibilla and her much more youthful lover.

The two poles of the erotic attraction are even more distinct than before: on the one hand, there is the woman, on her solitary pilgrimage, with her physical debility, her economic difficulties, her particular emotion and sexual needs; on the other there is the 'miraculous dawning' of a union, after a lengthy Calvary.

Death and emptiness still figure as the background, but take on the more realistic forms of lack of food and money, and ill-health. 'Ecstasy', for its part, emerges more clearly in its mystical aspect as a dream of resurrection.

Today I'm unwell. However physically healthy a woman is, she always remains vulnerable to this menstrual *malaise* and feels humiliated by it. No woman poet has yet achieved the heroic transcendence which would allow her to analyse and express this simultaneously animal and exalted state of being, these moments of suspended animation during which her spiritual life seems clouded over . . . that meagre contribution which women have succeeded in making to poetry is the result of a tension infinitely more stressful than the tension of virility; how much self-sacrifice is involved, I tell you, in any authentic attempt to confine one's creativity to the spirit, to escape from the blood. (Aleramo 1982a: 45)

In other words, between the feminine condition, viewed in its most physical dimensions, and the artistic quest, there is a violent dislocation, an almost insurmountable rift. Spiritual creation for a woman necessarily involves self-renunciation. Only by reneging on her own physicality can she make the necessary imaginary leap into the place of another. It is at this point that Sibilla begins to feel that life and writing (where 'writing' means 'lyric verse' or 'poetry') do not naturally combine, but involve a necessary tension and 'self-sacrifice'.

Amo dunque sono (1927) in fact marks the beginning of a different style of writing, a little closer to life, a little more distant from poetry, a style which finds its most complete expression in the *Diari*, and whose novelty was not at the time appreciated even by Sibilla herself. Thanks to the better sense of distance and diversity allowed her by this new mood of relative disenchantment, Sibilla is able to realize that love's 'sublime' quality is also its 'childishness': it is not so much a saint but a baby who undertakes the ascent of Calvary.

Do you love me? I know there are some things one doesn't ask. But tonight let me be a baby! You said 'what a baby you are – how changeable!' But you too changed, became tender, protective. So do you love me? (Aleramo 1982a: 47)

The absurdity of love is that it 'rises like a sheer precipice, like these bare rocks over the abyss'. The mystical element in the dream of harmonious reunion is perceived more clearly, but so too is its character as fiction, as imaginary creation. 'I write of them, you see, as if they were inventions of fantasy – unreal persons, skilful contrivances for my own delight, like the doll in the poem of Villiers de l'Isle Adam' (Aleramo 1982a: 126).

Ecstasy, the plenitude of perfect mutual understanding, is, in reality, silence:

> What man ever really knows what a woman experiences when he possesses her? What does he know of her desire or her exhaustion? And what does the woman ever know of the man? There is a silence between them, which I would like to term ancestral, if not directly animal, which from time immemorial has devalued the act of love, and brought it back down from the spiritual plane. (Aleramo 1982a: 128)

Sibilla's lonely struggle, for all its heroic impulses, reveals its actual fragility: the pursuit of self-sufficiency is an 'odious' imposition, which leaves one constantly at the mercy of one's nostalgia and desire for the presence of the other:

> There are days, consigned to the obscurity of one's diary, when even the strongest people, those most accustomed to solitude, give vent to something more faltering within them: 'this self-sufficiency – how odious it is. . . . Look, even the simplest gesture of picking a daisy as one walks by the edge of a stream . . . how one craves sometimes for another hand . . . for another hand . . . to pluck that flower for one!' (Aleramo 1982a: 136)

Aleramo's 'ultimate illusion', her love for Franco Matacotta (when he was 20, and she was 60), was a re-enactment of the mother-son relationship in which she had had her first experience of love.

That her dream of a perfect unity between the two of them, Franco and Sibilla, derives from this early experience, is evident from the beginning of the relationship. Once again, we come across the image of mutual devouring: real nourishment and growth for the man-son, the illusion of birth and rejuvenation for the woman-mother. The encounter started off as mutual fusion: they are plants nurtured on the same sap, she the 'great oak tree', he the 'young sapling', each plundering the resources of the other:

> While he drew breath and nourishment from me, from my spirit, from my immense experience, it was as if I meanwhile,

by some curious sorcery, had been invested with his tender years, and was tasting the pleasures and pains of his youth in a strange and continuous duplication of our personalities.

(Aleramo 1979a: 7)

But this image of a mutual imprisonment, wherein each acted as the other's warder, is belied in comments recorded not long afterwards by Franco:

If I look back over that period, I have to realize I was lying when I claimed to be wholly dominated by her. It was a pretence I let her believe. It was an alibi I created for myself, in order to secure greater control over her. It was I who intruded upon her life, who disturbed the placid calm of her years, who invaded her. And then I wearied of it. At that point, I was more than happy to seize the opportunity which the war provided to escape. (Aleramo 1979a: 269)

The son, whom she has nurtured to strength, returns to the society of men, while the mother, instead of discovering a new life in his, realizes she has done no more than sacrifice her own:

The real truth is that I feel orphaned by Franco. Not widowed, but orphaned . . . I find myself without roots, without sap, a pitiful, abandoned creature. . . .
I can't manage to find my inner freedom, my need for self-sufficiency. . . .
I am a block of ice this evening.

(Aleramo 1979a: 381, 52, 63)

With the loss of Franco, and of every other love for a man, Aleramo reveals the fundamental meaning of her dream of love:

I can't live without being essential to some other person. This is what lies at the heart of it. When Franco was here, right up until that last week of bitter frustration, there were times when it seemed to me, indeed I said as much to him, that his leaving would come as a relief; that I was longing for solitude and freedom, and that once restored to these former companions I would begin to work again. But as soon as I actually found myself alone, I realized the truth about love: that it is an attachment to someone to whom one thinks one is necessary. Or it is for a woman, at any rate, and also for those men in whom the feminine predominates. For eight years, I gave the whole of

myself to Franco . . . I perpetrated this act of sacrilege against
my individuality, because of the child who was drawing his
strength from mine. . . . Each day, I died and was reborn in
him, sometimes happily, sometimes unhappily, but always in
obedience to a fate, a law, and also, yes, to the call of a mysterious harmony whose music transcended every opposition.

(Aleramo 1979a: 290)

'Indispensability', however imaginary, is the only guarantee of
a continued attachment to others, of the power both to give and
to receive life. It reassures us of our right to childhood; it invites
us to expect a reward for the sacrifice, which, we think, entitles
us to some happiness in return for our suffering.

Love is self-abnegation and devotion, but it is also a claim to
maternal protection. The bond and affections of infancy are
experienced as a necessity of 'fate' or a 'law' of the human condition, but also as a 'mysterious harmony', in which the mother, or
perhaps an ideal original unity, is possessed, in illusion.

Surely it is no coincidence that it is in reference to her son that
Aleramo addresses (in her early novel, *A Woman*) her most precise and revealing question about love: 'Why did I so ludicrously
demand from him the love my life had always lacked?' (Aleramo
1979b: 149).

THE SADNESS WHICH IS FREEDOM

This notion of 'indispensability' can help us to understand why it
is that women find the experience of genuine autonomy and solitude so hard to come by, why they seldom achieve it, and why,
when they do, it is so often tainted by that sense of 'melancholy'
which descends in the absence of strong passions of either joy
or pain.

Even when she begins to recognize that something is changing
within her, and that this new experience and outlook on life are
finding expression in an equally novel style of writing, such as
we find in her *Diari*, Sibilla still clings with some part of herself to
her *grandiose conception*, to her dream of fulfilling her childhood
need in a perfect communion with a man.

Thus, if she can no longer prove indispensable to a man, at
least she can give herself over to an Idea:

Why not allow myself some pride in my commitment to the
Party . . . pride in an old age that can find all it needs in this
cause, that finds the courage to continue day after day, however exhausted, knowing how essential it is, how crucial an
element in the common struggle. . . .

Here I am alone in the silent house, resting . . . having just
read the issue of *Unità* with almost the whole of its third page
devoted to me . . . which means, perhaps, that upwards of a
million comrades were thinking of me this morning with affec-
tion.   (Aleramo 1978a: 327, 415)

Prima facie, this solitude, which is depicted as a kind of *heroic
resistance* and which goes together with an exalted image of herself as encompassing both death and renaissance, both impo-
tence and omnipotence, might seem to indicate an increase in
autonomy. In reality, however, it signals her ultimate incapacity
to engage herself in a true, actual existence, and to stand alone in
the face of life and death.

For the freedom she both wants and fears can be gained only at
the cost of a definitive break with a fantasized or actual childhood. It means withdrawal not only from the actual embrace of
real lovers, but from the arms of those imaginary creatures who
populate her dream of love.

The past! It is Christmas Eve. I make for home, elbowing my
way through the sluggish crowds, all in groups and couples.
. . . No woman is as alone as I am. My companion had to leave
me. . . . Even now I could find him down there in our tiny little
room illuminated by the white light of the lamp. But still this
lonely walk, on a night such as this, with my little parcel under
my arm – it saddens me. Perhaps, it's simply the memory of
childhood, of those Christmas Eves when my father used to take
me out for a stroll through the slowly emptying streets before
lunch, and I, holding on to his hand, felt what a small person I
was, how deserving of his strong support. Perhaps it is
womanly atavism. A woman finds it a good deal less easy than
a man to break with certain traditions, because there is such
sweetness and seduction for her in their *observance*. Occupying
as she does so central a place in the home, it is the woman,
almost exclusively, who feels the glow of these solemn rituals –
she and the children. . . . That she must forgo all these ancient
prerogatives, albeit in the interests of some superior gain, is a

cause of overwhelming sadness to her, of all that vague regret
one feels for something that has gone for ever.

(Aleramo 1978: 165)

In the light of this profound intuition, which makes us rethink
the destiny of both men and women, and likewise the desire that
binds them, albeit in different ways, to childhood, we are able to
see that the dream of love extends to more than erotic relations.
The search for a harmonization of 'natural differences', for a
union of male and female traditions, and for everything the social
order insists on segregating – this is the central question not only
of Sibilla's love-affairs, but of the heroic solitude to which she has
recourse in the wake of her earlier disillusionments.

Opposed to the 'sad' solitude of the woman, who slowly and
almost without realizing it, begins to renounce her claims to
childhood, there is the *omnipotent solitude* in which Sibilla placed
her hopes of self-generation over such a long period of her life.
Ecstasy, rather than the fusion of two persons in one, is the dream
of a birth, wonderful and propitious, from a 'divine duality' of
male and female, mother and father, which finally compensates
the woman for her historic mutilation and restores her stolen
childhood.

Who have I to thank for my strength? For the miracle I've so
long thought of myself as being? I've long been aware of the
conflict within me – between my mother's gentleness, and my
father's violence, between her melancholic discretion, and his
rebellious boldness, between my inclination to silence and my
urge to command an audience, between my servile devotion
and my instinct to dominate . . . the two always in perpetual
tension. My parents, I told myself, were profoundly mis-
matched – and in the divergence of their temperaments lay the
source of the incurable malady afflicting me. And again, I told
myself, that if the product of this calamitous union contained
within it something of value none the less, then that was a
wonder which one could not begin to fathom.

But one night, not so long ago, I was lying awake, as so
often, when I was struck by this thought, which came to me
with all the suddenness and certainty of a revelation. I'm not
sure, in fact, whether it was a thought or an imaginative vision
of some kind. But I found myself thinking, as in a reverie, of
the bond that had united my mother and father, of their love for

each other. I thought of each of them in their youth. I had been conceived out of the ecstasy and delirium of these two youthful, beautiful creatures, who had triumphed over every sadness. I was their first-born, the fruit of their joy, the fusion of their twin flames. They had loved each other because of their difference. They had flung their separate beings together for my sake, in order to give rise to the unique, whole person who was myself, a person who could combine their different selves, and could receive and cherish that fused life in its totality.

(Aleramo 1932: 4, 5, 6)

Whatever the particular image used to evoke this cathedral-like edifice of narcissism soaring above the 'cavernous existence' of the world it always refers us to a recomposition of the dualities of a masculine universe and is modelled symbolically on the male body and male desire. At one time, it is a 'sublime virgin', who unites within herself the softness of the maternal body and the fecund power of the man:

Men, they are, not heroes, who think of life as a cell within which they feel themselves more or less confined. Feverish prisoners, they react to their lot with resignation or with grim determination as the case may be. Pitiful creatures . . . understanding them, I loved them.   (Aleramo 1942: 184)

At another time, it is eternal 'nature' which encompasses within it the masculine and the feminine principles:

She is intelligence and love, wisdom and suffering, the lily of the valley haloed in light, the skylark ascending unscathed above the storm. . . .

A spirit which is both lost and regained, which is cast down by men as it is reanimated by them: that is my spirit, too, my aura. Is it the centre, or the ray which emanates? I don't know. They don't know. Or perhaps it is some kind of pollen? . . .

Who shall I now make fertile? These perfumes are seeds of the eternal sun.   (Aleramo 1932: 101, 172, 173)

And now again, it is the 'larva' watched over by silence, whose moment of birth is poetry, a triumphal 'entry' upon the 'mythical'.

At other times, Sibilla refers more explicitly to the myth of the Androgyne or that of Adam and Eve. Nor is it surprising, perhaps, given her particular passion and insight, that she sees herself in both Adam and the lover of Plato's myth, with their desire to be reunited with their feminine element.

The 'ideal of virility', whose image is such a constant component of Aleramo's ceaseless 'struggle for self-creation', a struggle which renders her both 'inhuman' and 'superhuman', which gives her the omnipotence of a god, but of a god who remains 'nameless' and 'realm-less', is bound up with that precise childhood memory to which she returns in the opening pages of *A Woman*: 'When I walked beside him along the city streets or in the countryside beyond the city walls, holding on to his hand for hours upon end, I felt extraordinarily elated' (Aleramo 1979b: 1).

If a woman is to be 'born', in the sense of undergoing a process of self-discovery throughout her life, then what is required is not only *completeness* but a synthesis of the maternal and paternal in which that 'birth' can find its source. This is why Sibilla tries to find in a man the basis for a duality in order that she herself may subsequently incorporate it within herself.

And it is this combined need to be both self-born and someone else's infant, to enjoy both autonomy and maternal protection, which gives rise to the *paradox of a law of survival* for which death is the source of life, submission that of dominion, pain that of joy; which gives the woman the illusion of bringing her own life into being even as her forces go to swell the life of another.

In the 'coldness' and 'grief' which she felt after Franco Matacotta abandoned her, Sibilla still clings to her dream of 'being held in the palm of his hand', still listens for a voice that will say 'stay here and rest for a moment'. Her freedom, her project of 'living for herself', requires her, by contrast, to think of herself as *alone*.

I rediscover the silence in me, the solitude, the possibility of writing again, and this deep sadness which is freedom, whose value one appreciates only in its absence. But some change has taken place in me. I don't know how to define it. I don't yet want to analyse it, I can't measure its scope or profundity. Only this I know for sure: I am no longer the same person I was when I was still waiting, as I was a month ago, for Franco to come back. And there has been a silent acceptance within me of this change. It has come about without feelings of either joy or distress – so strange.   (Aleramo 1978: 27)

It is in her *Diari*, and in particular her *Diario di una donna*, that she best describes this 'second life' with its 'silent current of thought and feeling', which a woman cannot translate into poetry without 'doing violence to herself', without 'dehumanizing' herself.

But difficult as it is for her to find means of valuing life in its reality, outside her dreams, it is equally difficult for her to recognize herself in what seems simply to record a period of waiting, a period within which she can only 'exist' rather than 'create'. 'Everything I come up against, every thought, must it be so evanescent? Can I no longer create, but merely exist?' (Aleramo 1978: 200).

When the 'heroic' ambition relaxes its hold and her dream reforms itself, it is no longer transfixed by the temporal immobility of an imagined existence, in which both 'sublime' exaltation and 'childlike' pathos are combined. She is then able to rediscover a 'profound sense of life' – the significance which life has at the moment when it is most distant.

> The sudden elation of throwing open the shutters and seeing the newly risen sun casting its dazzling beam over the sea. That joy in the present moment, which is a delight of the eye, but surely of the heart, too. The profound sense of life, the profound distance from life. Embrace it, dear heart, for ever, henceforth, until death.   (Aleramo 1978: 174)

It is surely no coincidence that Aleramo draws near to 'real autonomy' as a woman at precisely the moment when she is most distant from the world of her dreams – and thus closest to the reality of life and death.

6 Introduction to the script of the film *Scuola senza fine*

ADRIANA MONTI

Translated by Giovanna Ascelle

After I had been working with a particular group of housewives for a year we started shooting the film *Scuola senza fine* (literally, 'School without end') almost casually, in 1979. I was able to get equipment free of charge and money to pay for the film was made available. The women had taken the '150 Hours' course and had been awarded the completion of secondary school diploma in 1976. But they were reluctant to go back to spending their afternoons ironing or playing cards. So first we devised new seminars on literature, the body and the image.

Rediscovering the pleasure of reading and studying was like reliving their adolescence. It was important for them to have a teacher to whom they could tell in writing what they had done and thought, their past history and plans for the future. The teacher of the diploma course was someone who listened to them and made them think: Lea Melandri, who came from the Women's Movement where she was considered a fine theorist and had been a promoter firstly of the *gruppo dell'inconscio* (see p.7) and then of the Sexuality and Writing group. She was consequently familiar with issues related to the unconscious, to women's relationships with each other, and to the individual's relationship with culture and knowledge. She was able to strengthen the women's expressive potential and transformed the adult education course into a study and research group which was later joined by more teachers and new students.

Watching the project develop was like uncorking a champagne bottle. The women's writing matured and began to flow and sparkle while Lea, whose book *L'infamia originaria* was about to be published, did not write anything else for several years. The women students, encouraged first by Lea and the discovery of Freud, then by the other teachers and by science, philosophy, and linguistic analysis (visual, written, and body languages), filled page after page of their writing pads and exercise books (or in Amalia's case, loose sheets), with personal reflections on culture, themselves, their families, nature, and feelings.

The group changed in the course of time and in 1981 it became a graphics co-operative. In the early years, and during the shooting of the film (1979–81), it was important for the women to be able to socialize without the usual local prejudices. Lunches, dinners, dances, parties, and going to discos were the most frequent forms of entertainment.

The film shows how the women related to each other at that time and the special closeness each woman felt for every other – perhaps because they came from the same place, or shared the same ideals and way of thinking, or, simply, because they were fond of each other. For many women, rediscovering the mother-teacher relationship meant being able to express thoughts which had often been undervalued or disregarded (most of the housewives attending the course had given up their education to go to work or had not been able to make use of the knowledge they had already, because they stayed at home after getting married). The opportunity to relive that relationship in a learning situation stimulated a very interesting kind of writing and thought. At first, the women's unfailing ability to get to the heart of philosophical and scientific issues used to take us by surprise. Their writing shows an independent way of thinking which is not dazzled by long words or intimidated by theory; they used to play with theories or use them as magic formulas, but always to approach a question to which there was no answer. This approach to culture caused a number of difficulties but this is not what the film is about. The task of tracing that part of the story can be left to subsequent writing and other documents. The film merely records the initial part of the work and recreates its atmosphere. The social occasions indicate how individuals related to the group, while individual pieces of writing show us how thinking develops and unfolds – at a kitchen table in the middle of the night, on a stage, or facing a blank drawing sheet, while dancing, or looking at window-box plants that evoke the countryside, or walking home.

Every now and then, during those three years, I used to take the camera and film. Then I gave it all up and did not touch the material for two years.

The shooting of the first part of the film was undertaken collectively. But then everybody lost interest in it. I decided to finish it on my own and this is how the second part, the individual chapters, took shape. I found it painful to contain in language the intense experience of our lives together but I had to convey it as best I could. This is what I said to myself every time I shut myself away to edit. But working on the film was like operating on a hypothetical, complex, and multi-faceted maternal body for which I had to find a shape, especially in the second part of the film where I had to look directly at each woman in turn. I used editing the film in my free evenings as an alibi to hold my anxieties and anguish at bay. At last, in February 1983, the final copy was printed.

Title: *Scuola senza fine*
Film in 16 mm, black and white (negative) with optical sound
Length: 40 minutes
Production: Adriana Monti and '150 Hours' course teachers
Photography (Amalia: kitchen and theatre) and editing
    assistance: Angelo Cordini
Conceived and directed by Adriana Monti
Made with the collaboration of: Lea Melandri, Amalia Molinelli,
Ada Flaminio, Antonia Daddato, Teresa Paset, Rina Aprile,
Micci Toniolo, Paola Mattioli, Maria Martinotti.

7 *Script of the film* Scuola senza fine

Translated by Fausta Daldini Einhorn

AMALIA

The '150 Hours Project' is a victory that the workers won after years of struggle. Until recently only workers of large companies could attend, but since 1976 it has been made available to housewives and retired workers as well. It is called '150 Hours' because workers are given 150 hours' paid leave by their employers to attend classes. The full course is 350 hours. At the Via Gabbro school there were courses four times a week, three hours a day.

What happens at the school? To start with each participant talks about her/his life and writes about it in whatever way is personally possible. Italian is taught by reading and group discussions of current affairs. As well as being a place to receive education, the school is also a meeting place where participants can discuss their problems. Housewives are called on to get out of their homes and take some time to think about themselves: they never regret it. The course lasts for one year at the end of which participants receive a completion of secondary school diploma.

LEA MELANDRI

SPRING 1979

A room of one's own can be used for many purposes. Virginia

Lea Melandri (second from the right in the first photograph) with participants in the '150 Hours' course of Affori

Woolf made the best hypothesis: it is a springboard to reality. Preferring not to think of myself as a cultured woman, I have locked up inside a room of my own the true object of my desires: to think, to read, to write, although I have thought a lot and read and written much less. The '150 Hours Project' is the Left's most original and interesting creation of recent years. You go into a classroom, as I did, and find twenty women having a lively discussion about town planning and overcrowding in cities, while in the next room a group of chemical workers talk about love, in a cloud of cigarette smoke.

I wanted you all to find out in three months what it has taken me years of suffering to learn. I didn't even have time to understand what I meant to you. I was aware that I was a catalyst for your personal development and this gave me energy. I enjoyed myself (on the way home in the evening I would sing to myself). I don't know if I ever told you, but you could probably tell anyway. . . . One day, at the end of the course, I went into a shop with Pina and bought some perfume. I heard her say: 'You are a woman after all!' I often thought about this comment because even though we had had so many discussions, I managed to pass myself off as an asexual being, who thinks and makes others think, but hides her daily life. But I made up for this lack. Last summer I managed to take some of you to Romagna to meet my mother and father, and visit my home village. Our relationship became more balanced and now we can dance together and even write together.

I was very envious of your felicitous style of writing, which is so direct and free in its images, without being sentimental. Meanwhile by myself at home, I was finishing writing a book that you all found almost incomprehensible.

NOVEMBER 1977

What is writing?
Is it a constraint? A way of avoiding suffering? A substitute for a walk or a love-affair? Is it an omnipotent dream of meaning something to a lot of different people and being known in a lot of different places? Or is it the pleasure of tempting the imagination or the freedom to hide behind a disguise?

Why do I write?
During my childhood I wrote to avoid hearing what was going on

at home, to avoid seeing the monotonous changes of the countryside, to get myself over holiday-time depression when the
days never seemed to end.

Behind any kind of writing, be it romantic or theoretical, private or public, lies an anxious search for somebody who is not
there. Maybe the mind and words have, for too long, been
opposed to the body. Maybe we cannot recognize the body
which can be glimpsed behind the words as our own.

On a grey Sunday in Milan it is better to sleep than write. . . .

TERESA

It was my younger son who sent in the registration form after
he heard the youngest one telling me to get out of the house and
go to school. You see, I was upset because my husband could not
attend the school. . . . My son kept saying: 'Mum, don't stay
at home staring at the furniture, get out.' He practically pushed
me out of the door and I went out and came back a different
person.

It is wonderful to be with people. This is a school where you
can talk to people.

ADA. Talk and be listened to.
TERESA. I felt very nervous about it.
LEA. Teresa, how did you get to know Amalia?
TERESA. I saw this country woman and realized her reasons for
coming to the school were probably the same as mine. I come
from a village and I used to be ashamed of it, but now I like it. I
am a peasant. . . . Amalia was sitting next to us and she began
to talk. I liked her calmness. It made me feel comfortable. You
see, these are the women friends I value, women who are sincere and interested, and want to know about me. I like people
as they are. I like to tell them jokes and keep them happy. They
should be the same with me.
AMALIA. It's great to get to know a lot of well-educated people. I
enjoy talking to them. I can't be myself when I have to talk to
people who don't understand anything. I end up letting them
think that they are right even when I know that they are
wrong.
TERESA. Since people have a lot of ideas in their heads, you have

to find out if they understand the meaning of what they say. I like these things to be clear. I laugh, I joke, but I think.

AMALIA. Teresa, you are always afraid of people passing judgement on you.

TERESA. It's happened so many times that I feel inhibited now.

ADA. Your cheerfulness has never been understood.

TERESA. Knowing you has been wonderful. You understand me, you let me be myself, let me say stupid things sometimes.

AMALIA. When I was at home and there was no school, I didn't know what to do with myself. What would I do? So, I started looking through books. The day we read *Dalla parte delle bambine* I ran into difficulties because I didn't know words like 'a n t h r o p o l o g y'. If I hadn't gone to this school I would never have known the meaning of words like anthropology, psychology, or sociology, although sociology is a bit more familiar.

TERESA. Watch out though: people use psychologist, psychology, and psychosis as if they were one and the same word!

AMALIA. You have to be a great thinker to understand these things and by thinking it over and over we'll find ourselves unthought! [laughs]

LEA. Amalia is the real backbone of the class! The curious thing is that you, Ada, ever joined this group, these forces of nature.

ADA. It's because they had a lot of things to say and I had none. When Amalia was writing anything she would write a lot, it was as if she was writing for me too. She had words for all the memories I had that at the time I could not express.

TERESA. Lea was a woman who would think first, then speak. I liked her long silences. I didn't know how to talk. A lot of what I said was nonsense. It all used to come spilling out. The truth was that we were both terribly inhibited.

LEA. You've told me that I'm shy.

AMALIA. Yes, you are shy. That's why I said it.

LEA. First you told me that I was shy. Then you told me that I was aggressive, but in what way?

TERESA. You would always encourage us to talk and read.

LEA. Didn't I talk a lot?

TERESA. We didn't let you talk much.

LEA. That's right, I used to listen.

TERESA. Do you know why we talked so much? Because we had found the right environment, after thirty years of waiting.

AMALIA. In spite of your quiet listening you said a lot.

LEA. Yes, I used to talk a lot too, although I can't really remember what it felt like. From what you are telling me now, I realize that I was very much present during those discussions, although I cannot now remember what they were like. What I remember is having fun, dancing, and laughing. But I know that I worked very hard with you on a lot of aspects of thought and discussion and on the condition of women. Although I was there, I cannot picture myself among you. Yesterday I asked Amalia to tell me how she saw me. And what she saw was the intellectual, the teacher, and I took this as confirmation that I was very much present, especially to make you all think and talk.

AMALIA MOLINELLI

I will always remember the early mornings, when we used to set out in the dark to gather the meagre harvest. I would hear the cry of the owl . . . OOH . . . OOH . . . OHOOOOO. I had never heard such a horrible sound. I was scared and asked my father what it was. 'It's an owl, of course.' But the cry was so loud that it sounded like a person moaning. Maybe there was a time when people didn't know that it was a night bird hooting and thought it was a ghost. . . . Once we reached the field we had to load the hay and mind the cows which were always trying to get out and trespass into the other little fields. And when that happened, we would get yelled at, sworn at, and insulted. But we were poor and we had to swallow the insults. What else could we do?

A time came when people began to realize that the universe was beautiful as well as frightening. They began to understand its harmony. Myths were born that told tales, in allegorical images, of how people used their reason to discover the mysteries of nature and the obscure origins of the world.

I believe that myths are enchanting fairy-tales produced by ignorance. People invented myths for protection: as a way of putting themselves in the hands of a saint or god and imploring its protection. This idea makes one feel calm . . . thoughts fly high up above and the imagination takes over. It is reassuring but it is not true. Inside I feel this protection that stays with me even when I am walking along dangerous, steep paths. When I had to cut grass on steep slopes where not even goats would go, I would keep saying to myself, 'Lord help me, help me', and it made me feel calm and sure that I would not slip. Today they say that this is only autosuggestion, but maybe this practice has been passed down from our ancestors as a myth of divine help: in the same way as, for the child, the mother's protection is the only protection.

Every Friday we plan and organize for a two-year study programme for women who are living in a blissful state of ignorance and know nothing! At each meeting the teachers give us a list of subjects including chemistry, physics, biology, and art. Somebody always asks nervously about the difficult things we will have to study.

It is wonderful to know so many things and to be able to talk to people who have studied. Sometimes they ask me how I know so much. They look at me a little astonished when I tell them that it is because I go to school. When they ask why I go to school, I feel very good telling them that it is because I want to make my own contribution to culture.

So many things came to my mind when I first looked at pictures of the atom. I didn't know where to start. For instance, I could begin to tell a story imagining that molecules could talk and could discuss things while they produced carbon dioxide and oxygen. It seemed to me that they wasted a lot of energy and ran the risk of splitting into atoms! Everything would end up in total chaos, a hydrogen bomb. I wondered what the molecules knew that could make them go in for such desperate and chaotic exchanges without rhyme or reason. In their world, the transmitter transmits at top volume, the receiver doesn't receive and everyone talks and nobody understands.

There are many kinds of life sentences. I am a poor woman who was doomed from birth: my mother really wanted a boy. I have only just understood why I felt rejected. It makes me laugh a little! I got married in Holy Year, 1950. I have no idea what was so holy about that year since there has been nothing holy about my marriage: it's all been just hard work. I married into a family of poor sharecroppers.

In those days we had to work very hard but we loved each other, we cared for each other. There was more human warmth. We lived in a village where we always helped each other out when there was need. Today I live in the city. There is a lot of talk about the community and social relations. But whose social relations are we talking about? City people are used only to thinking about themselves and they keep all their problems to themselves. And the woman always has to take responsibility for family problems.

When I go to bed I cannot relax, my brain carries on an endless conversation. It is like closed circuit TV that can't be turned off! Then my fantasies stop and I turn off the 'improbable' only to wake up the next morning exhausted and still thinking. Who am I to be so rebellious? Am I the imaginary of my imagination?

I reached the age of 50 without ever realizing what it meant to create culture or be interested in knowledge. The more I know, the more I realize how little I know. Anyway, it's nice to find out about new things, to read, and to listen to people who know more than I do and can express it well.

I find myself with half a century of life behind me, a life spent working, never imagining that there could be anything apart from work. I felt a void inside of me. There were days when I wondered what I had done with my life. I had done a lot of constructive work but all for other people, never for myself. So I wondered what could be the use of living such a useless life that has no purpose! The same things, the same faces, the same boring housework, the same conversations all the time. Why not try to change my life! So I learned about culture and in four years of school I have written a book. It will be quite confused, but people will understand it anyway: the title will be 'Amalia's vagabond thoughts'. From the title people will understand that my search for something developed slowly from conversations we had in class, from bits of biographical memories about my hectic life. And now a book has been written by an ordinary woman: what will 'high society' say? No matter what happens, I wanted to scribble down my ideas. If people aren't interested I don't give a damn: I will always be the same Amalia. A very strange woman who is a bit vain, who always thinks as she walks past a mirror 'Well, I'm a bit fat, but I'm beautiful just the same.'

ANTONIA DADDATO

It took courage for me to join the '150 Hours Project'. I was over 40 and had three children. Once I had made the decision, I began to get palpitations, for example on the first day of school, which was a big thing for many of us. After the first week we built up some sort of mutual trust and understanding.

My problems started at the end of the course when I realized that it would be very difficult for me to go on studying the things I had just begun to learn about. I didn't want to lose touch with the people I was in dialogue with. But it is not easy to get together with other women without the excuse of school or work. It means facing a series of difficulties which should not be under-estimated. If someone has never dreamed of doing anything without the agreement of her husband, children, or relatives, her family puts up a lot of resistance if she starts to do so. But even worse, after a few stolen hours away from the household and its routine, one often finds that the habit of not doing anything for oneself has built up inhibitions. It is a habit that generates anxiety but that one would like to get rid of quickly. But how can women quickly free their bodies and minds from something that has been building up inside them for millennia?

ADA FLAMINIO

I think about my life and I don't find myself. 'A bonding relation-ship with the love object'.

Once again, as Lea is talking, I think about my relationship with my children: a bonding relationship where the thought of separation never crossed my mind. Rationally, I had thought out many correct theories about their autonomy, their indepen-dence, their right to control their own lives and stand on their own feet. These had remained purely theoretical because when the time came I felt lost – a void, panic, anguish. Then questions began to occur to me: who am I? am I here? do I exist?

The other day my husband was telling the story of our married life. A fine story. I listened and at a certain point I couldn't believe what I heard: I wasn't in that story. There was only him, alone with his fine story. He had never seen my loneliness, my suffering, my dissatisfaction. I was struck by this and it made me think a lot. But it is true. If I think about my life up to now, I can-not put my own story together, only that of my sons. It is me for them, with them, in an intense dialogue, the three of us alone, all in one. The essence of myself transplanted in them. What about me? Why didn't I keep anything for myself? What have I done for myself? And why does the thought of separation make me feel as if I was dying? Why is there this feeling of void in my past?

JANUARY 1980

Today we had a long discussion about how the course is going and a lot of things came to light. I arrived home more than an hour ago. I cannot do anything. My feelings and emotions are making me feel very confused.

I make room on the table among the mess of scattered shopping bags, tangerine peels, tea cups . . . nothing matters, I want to write, maybe writing will help me free myself and give me some understanding.

THOUGHTS AT THE END OF A CHEMISTRY COURSE

Doing a chemistry course made me realize that it was the evolution of human thought that attracted me to science.

What fascinates me is that in the beginning humans had this incredible ability to be one with nature. Later, when their thinking evolved due to their scientific discoveries, they changed their symbols in order to represent this new objective reality. Today, in spite of all their scientific achievements, modern humans still need a subjective interpretation of love and hate, fear of life and death.

TERESA PASET

Historically, motherhood has been such an integral part of a woman's experience that her life became one with that of her child. A woman who has given birth sees her child as a complement to herself. She is her son's warder (meant in a positive sense) and the prisoner of her motherhood at the same time.

She spends her life in her son's shadow, she feels a morbid love for him, she defends him from everything and everybody. In certain cases she prevents him from growing up, because she has not found her own dimension and continues to subject herself to the role of mother-servant, which is so alienating as to make her life unmanageable. Today a lot of young people are free from prejudice and think women and mothers are capable of achieving great things. They help them get out of this psychological prison. They encourage each woman to be herself and to find a purpose in life which is consistent with her character.

We often resist becoming involved in social issues for fear of being judged by other women, who are themselves slaves of these same prejudices. In spite of having left school originally so many years ago, all the students in my class participate enthusiastically and feel younger in spirit as a result. This group has built up a climate of sincere participation and harmony.

LEA MELANDRI

L'INFAMIA ORIGINARIA[1]

For a woman, the problem of survival never changes even in adulthood. It is the need to be nourished as well as to nourish; it is the need to be loved as well as to love. One can escape from dependency, from the expectation that somebody else will guarantee one's life, but women never feel they are allowed to play with freedom.

Man's privilege includes the fact that he can choose to be *hungry* while allowing himself to *play*. It is a balance between survival and pleasure which is based on a separation. It is a balance which allows him to avoid suffering. Unlike man, in the absence of pleasure, woman is *forced* to feel *hungry* while at the same time she feels *ashamed* of it.

In a woman's daily life, survival becomes an experience without apparent time or history. The point of arrival and of departure remains the original one: a kind of fixity and immobility that are the cause of the paralysis and the mutilation of 'doing' (action). It is only through great effort that a woman succeeds in making man's work her own. Her energies continue, obstinately, to be tied to a search for an ideal mother's love, a love burdened with guilt and fear. The last resort is motherhood: her own transformation from abandoned daughter to generous mother. The experience of maternal abandonment/betrayal forces the woman to turn to a man for proof of her own existence and her own value. She therefore finds herself deprived of her life and deprived of the meaning that her life could have. She is forced to redirect her impulses. She must keep them within the limits that man imposes in order to satisfy his own impulses. She measures and mystifies her desires to avoid repeating the original experience of abandonment.

NOTE

1 This ('The Original Disgrace') is the title of the book Lea Melandri was writing while teaching the course.

8 On the margins of feminist discourse: the experience of the '150 Hours Courses'

GIULIANA BRUNO AND MARIA NADOTTI

Translated by Jude Bloomfield in association with Material Word

The writings and video compilations of Paola Melchiori, Giulia Alberti, and Lea Melandri are the outcome of collective research on women and the cinema. Together with the experience of the Affori School and the Gervasia Broxon Co-operative, recorded in Adriana Monti's film *Scuola senza fine* (literally, 'School without end') they form part of the work carried out during the '150 Hours Courses' between 1974 and 1982. We consider it important to trace the broad outlines of their history since the interest and originality of this discourse, compared to Anglo-American feminist film theory, lie not not only in the texts as such, but particularly in their political and cultural context and in the process which produced them.

To understand these experiences and set them in their context it is essential to go back as far as 1974, the beginning of the study course entitled '150 Hours'.

In Italy the early 1970s was an explosive period of political and social transformation. Following the 'Italian economic miracle', consciousness of the change in the balance of forces between capital and labour influenced political and trade-union behaviour especially in the industrial field. This consciousness was to cause periodic outbursts of an increasingly direct nature throughout the 1960s, culminating in 1968 in the student movement (a phenomenon comparable to May in France and West Germany), and in what has been called the *autunno caldo* (hot autumn) in 1969. This was a period of hard-fought struggle by workers for specific political objectives which, for the first time in the post-war period, were definitely not reformist. They struggled not only for wage increases but also, and above all, to change their working conditions. The crucial demands shifted to: hours of work, workers' representation in the factory, conditions in the workplace, health and safety, control of the labour process and production cycle. These demands all tackled the issue of workers' control over companies' mode of production. While specific objectives (for example, control of the pace of the assembly line, the provision or improvement of canteens, the provision of a day-care service for workers with children of pre-school age, the adjustment of public transport timetables to factory working) may seem limited, their political import was not, and they certainly affected the quality of the workers' lives. By the end of the 1960s these were among the typical objectives of a movement which had become more political than economistic and, as a theoretical starting-point, challenged capitalist organization of the workers' time.

A profound transformation in the relation of workers to trade unions was produced by this political movement. The old form of trade-union representation which had grown up at the end of the Second World War and become entrenched in the period of economic reconstruction of the country, was based on the principle of delegation by the workers to their elected representatives. The rigid and selective principle of delegation corresponded to the employers' logic, and was merely aimed at defending workers' rights through a work contract. This modus operandi now proved to be outmoded and inadequate in the light of the new awareness. The desire to be direct protagonists in their own lives without the intercession of mediators was, in fact, one among many voiced by the workers' movement in the years of the 'Italian economic miracle'. It was encouraged by the upsurge of the student movement and by a new conception of political and trade-union activity as a form of direct, collective assembly. Concepts which were traditionally repressed by the political thinking of the western Left and labour movement, such as subjectivity/affectivity, and the body, burst on to the Italian trade-union political scene and upset its boundaries. At the end of the 1960s, the old assumption that mediation was the means of improving workers' conditions in the factory was on the way out. The movement of 1969 adopted the premise that there could be no mediation between the working class and capital. Rather than calling for workers' control, it undertook to find ways of workers dominating the labour process. Above all, it posited work as something which concerned not only the factory but the whole society: the pace of life was not seen as determined by the hours of work or the wage; the conditions and pace of work were now seen as reflected in other aspects of life such as the home, 'spare-time' pursuits, the family, study, health and personal relations.

In 1974, in this revitalized environment, one of the most interesting and original of workers' achievements in our recent past was established. This was the '150 Hours Courses': courses in basic literacy and courses leading to elementary and secondary school diplomas. Initially they were available to only two groups of industrial workers, the metal and chemical workers. The workers won this concession from their employers as a contractual obligation, provided free and in factory time, and the Italian state committed itself to organize, fund, and recognize them as regular courses of study. Effectively lasting 350 hours within a time-span of about six months, the '150 Hours Courses' acquired this inaccurate name because originally only 150 hours were granted as paid leave in working hours to be spent at college. Workers had to make up the rest on an individual basis, from their free time. The project was, in any case, a way of implementing the aim of reducing working hours and granting the workers more self-determination and freedom in the use of their time. Another major innovation of the scheme was that the courses were not aimed at training or retraining workers for their current work activity, nor were they refresher courses based on the present or future needs of production. Workers returned to school to study for their own benefit, not for production benefits, with teachers recruited in the normal way through the regular channels of the Ministry of Education. The aim was to retrieve what they had been deprived of at the proper time, to work less and think about their own conditions of life and work.

The factory was not excluded from the courses but appeared as an object of study and analysis. It was approached with new means of interpretation and new methods which were explicitly partisan, subjective, and open to question. To give some examples: the organization, pace, and methods of production became objects of research, for the purpose of assessing their impact on workers' physical and mental health. The work environment became a compulsory field of enquiry, in order to understand its material effects (contamination, environmental pollution, industrial accidents, the relationship between physical or psychic stress and behavioural disturbance, etc.). Wages also became a starting-point for research that aimed at a broader, overall analysis of the economic mechanisms that regulate life in Italian society. These included pensions, the wage indexation system, health insurance, the alternation of inflation and deflation, devaluation, etc.

Furthermore a large part of the courses was devoted to what was defined as the 'lived experience' of those attending the school. Workers of all ages from 20 to 60 came to the school. They were mainly southerners and often illiterates, people who had years of work experience, histories of emigration, experience of serious cultural and linguistic discrimination, and of political and trade-union struggle. It was not possible to leave out such significant backgrounds. The personal provided the reason for, and the object of, the process of acquiring knowledge. Not only because it dictated its rhythms and modes but also because the personal was seen as the inescapable raw material of the cognitive itinerary.

The political and social history of contemporary Italy was approached from a new angle, as an object of historical, sociological, and political enquiry starting from the life histories of course members. From being protagonists of events which they had experienced privately (such as leaving school early, illiteracy, leaving the land, moving to the city, and enduring the linguistic confusion of changing their everyday speech from dialect to the standard Italian of the industrial cities) they learnt in class to recognize and affirm these events as components in a collective history and in History itself. Phenomena which were considered private were acknowledged in their historical public dimension.

As will now be apparent, the impact of the '150 Hours Courses' was not only felt in the factory and trade-union political structure and society. It sent shock waves through the educational system itself and its languages, methodologies, and myths. It forced an in-depth enquiry into the nature of the pedagogic relationship and into the adequacy of cognitive theories to deal with a didactic experience in which the role of the teacher was questioned. Ultimately this entailed reversing the roles of student and teacher and creating a new work structure which was simultaneously practical and intellectual. It had to allow the teacher-student relation to become an area for research, for the exchange and circulation of different 'savoirs', rather than being a one-way transmission of knowledge and ready-made information.

Between 1974 and 1976 the '150 Hours' were expanded to include not only all categories of workers but also the unemployed, housewives, and pensioners, who similarly received a minimum wage for attending. In a theoretico-political practice which questioned the relationship between knowledge and power and highlighted 'savoirs mineurs', the innovative approach and content of the courses paid off as soon as women began to join en masse. Thus we come to our theme of women and the cinema. The women, whether students or teachers, brought to the courses not only a personal history and female sensibility, but also a consciousness which had meanwhile been heightening and finding expression in the more explicitly political context of the Women's Movement. The feminist practice of consciousness-raising, self-help, and *gruppi dell'inconscio* (see p.7) spilt over naturally and spontaneously into the '150 Hours Courses', whenever women teachers and groups of women students met.

Important experiences of collective discussion grew out of these gatherings, on themes such as health, the family, motherhood, and sexuality. They also gave rise to original formulations on the nature of the relationship to the female teacher figure who was an equal as a woman, but was felt to be superior as a cultured person with intellectual skills denied to others. Participants observed the dynamics which occur in a school community: subordination, dependence, envy, and jealousy, and the attribution of power, responsibility, and trust to others, with subsequent fantasies of death and displacement. Then they began to outline a series of theoretical hypotheses on the relation to the self and on the interaction that a school environment automatically induces, thus acquiring a groundwork and a sense of how to proceed to make use of the cognitive concepts derived from literature, science, communications, and the body of psychoanalytic theory as fields of study or analytical tools.

Undoubtedly the most original and rewarding result of women's participation in the '150 Hours Courses' took place at the school in Via Gabbro in Affori, on the outskirts of Milan. From 1974 to 1982, the same group of teachers (including Alberti, Melandri, Melchiori, and Monti) and students underwent a uniquely deep, long-lasting, and creative experience that went beyond the bounds of the '150 Hours Courses'. It developed into a project funded by the EEC, resulting in the formation of a complete self-managed graphics co-operative, 'Gervasia Broxon'.

Alongside the '150 Hours Courses' covering elementary and secondary-school education, the 'Monographic 150 Hours Courses' were established. They offered participants the same benefits as other courses, of paid leave and free tuition, but they were run in a university setting and granted no formal qualification at the end. These were personal and formative experiences which, as far as the women were concerned, most frequently took the form of research into subjectivity and identity, sometimes without the mediation of an identifiable object of study. These were genuine consciousness-raising groups, except that the principle was modified by the presence of one or more group leaders who were responsible for drawing conclusions from the collective work and publicizing it outwards after a given period of time.

A third group experience which originated in the framework of the '150 Hours Courses' took place at the same time as this. The teachers, particularly women, set up what have come to be known as 'Training support courses for teachers'. These are workshops and support groups only for those involved in teaching the '150 Hours Courses'.

The first Training support group for '150 Hours Courses' women teachers, in which Lea Melandri and Paola Melchiori participated, was founded in Milan in 1976 as a consciousness-raising group. There were no experts and the group was run collectively. Its hallmark, a result of making it open to women only, was the opportunity it gave to participants to describe their own teaching experience in the light of the mother-child relationship and of sexuality. (This is not to say that the problem is absent from men's experience, but that women feel it with particular urgency and as a more pressing priority.) For many women teachers, teaching does not provide adequate protection against the vulnerability or desire which enables their private life to be invaded, above all in a school like this one, which gives a lot of space to the personal. Intense involvement, passion, tiredness, the student-teacher relationship as a whole, show traces of, and cause emotional and sexual subtexts and tensions – an experience that the group was committed to recognizing and analysing in the first place.

The following year, however, the group set itself a research project: women and writing. At first they had tried to outline the problems of a woman teacher, then they had tried to grasp the relationship between the woman who teaches and the one who learns. But narration and analysis of experience no longer sufficed. They decided to analyse together an 'objective' material, the course members' plans of work and collections of writing, so that everyone could articulate those aspects of the experience which had been silenced, censored, or repressed in the verbal account. In fact, the writings proved very revealing about the complexity of the relationship between the woman who has studied and transmits culture and the woman who comes from a different social and psychological background characterized by family, children, housework, the factory, lack of education, etc. Furthermore, these writings give a clearer picture of some disagreeable and irritating female defences, often more marked among educated women, in tension between a sense of 'lack' or 'matriarchal omnipotence'. They also shed light on the workings of unconscious fantasies which draw on the traditional ways in which 'male' and 'female' have been symbolized.

In the Women and Writing group, and especially in the training courses which followed, a desire became increasingly evident to let the woman within the teacher figure emerge as a person in her own right, searching for ways of expressing herself or, at any rate, of taking a more active and direct part. (By this time, the teacher figure had been almost totally called into question, as there was some inkling of the maternal relationship of fullness/ emptiness, the 'comprehensive', all-encompassing embrace of someone who would rather be 'comprehended' herself, the implosion, etc., implicit in the role.)

In the third year, following an internal logic, the group turned to photography. Course practice was, by now, less influenced by the principles of the formative period, and, for the first time, it was decided to seek out a woman expert in the field, the film-maker Adriana Monti, who led the group. Members photographed each other, and became protagonists in the most direct way possible, by problematizing and staging the mise en scène of the original, primary form of narcissistic pleasure. Asking questions about liking and disliking one's own ego, they constructed a self-image, seeing one's own reflection in the other, mirroring each other. The search for female identity starts at this zero degree, which is simultaneously the lowest and most sophisticated social achievement (see advertising modes), and the first and most problematic aspect of women's personal experience (examine the insecurity that women feel about their appearance, their need for reassurance, their fears about use of their physical beings, etc.).

The photography group provided a moment of both technical achievement and play. At about the same time, Adriana Monti was shooting the film *Scuola senza fine* in Affori with students from the '150 Hours Courses' at Via Gabbro, where much the same thing was happening. The women who participated were finding out what it was like to be in front of the camera as protagonists, actresses. They were both gratified and disturbed at being looked at through the all-seeing eye of the camera with its power to reproduce their image and 'exhibit' a private life.

The following year the 'Training support course for "150 Hours Courses" women teachers' was modified further. The research theme changed to women and cinema and continued on these lines, and on a collective basis, for three years. Giulia Alberti joined Adriana Monti as course leader. The aim was to work on a language or text such as a film text which has specific structure and try to understand in each case the ways in which the cultural and technical construction of the film connected and merged with the sentimental, emotional, imaginary, and reflective experiences of the person watching. Particular attention was given to the image of woman as perceived at the juncture between the filmic text and the spectator's eye.

The course in the first year (1979–80) began under the title 'The cinema as representation: the place of the female in Hollywood cinema'. The representation of the female figure in classical Hollywood cinema was considered with particular reference to spatial and temporal organization and point of view, in order to define the position of the female figure in the juncture of narrative process and reading of a film.

In the second year, the work moved on to more recent cinema, with the study of films that were particularly concerned with subjectivity, including those of Resnais, Oshima, and Tarkovsky. The research continued in terms of cinematic effect, by investigating the type of imaginary figurations the cinema constructs. The group worked on the imaginary construction of masculinity and femininity, within and beyond the man/woman distinction. It dwelt particularly on the female protagonist as a male projection and on the assumption by the female spectator of a male point of view and desire. By asking themselves questions about the aspects that make up the pleasure of viewing a film for the female spectator, they did research on the imaginary world of the female figure and on the fascination it exerts. At stake was a definition of female pleasure.

Activity in the third year centred on preparations for producing a film. Doing critical research had indicated the need to realize certain intuitions through practical work, both to register the work that had been done, and to make it available to the outside world. It was considered appropriate to use the same cinematic language which enables the female spectator to relive the fascination and pleasure of viewing, interspersing it, however, with distanciation effects which make the devices of cinematic construction manifest. A series of compilation videos grew out of this and they were presented at the conference in New York. They were made individually by the women who participated in the course, to document their critical journey, seeking to retrace the trajectory of fascination open to critical female spectatorship. The compilation was intended to find answers to questions such as the following: what does the fascination of the female spectator derive from? what is its nature? what codes of representation does it draw on? what psychic mechanisms does it play on and which does it expose? what desires and lack does it rely on and which does it stimulate? To decide the structure of her film, each woman wrote a story. Several film sequences taken from the classical Hollywood repertoire, the locus of fascination *par excellence*, and from experimental films, several of which were directed by women, served as the raw material. This was an exercise in textual reading and analysing, and in identifying the moments of fascination in its genesis. At the same time, it was an exercise in writing, as they rewrote the texts by correlating these moments of fascination in the various films, through a process of deconstructive montage.

Therefore, the cognitive process which developed from the

experience of the '150 Hours' gave rise not only to a rich 'oral history', but to written texts and film texts. What is perhaps more important, it launched a research project and brought about a change in the relationship between the object, or product of knowledge, and its mode of production and circulation.

Let us leave Lea Melandri to comment on the didactic aspect of the experience of the discourse which she and the others produced:

The first and most obvious outcome of the experiment, which emerged from the 'Training support courses for teachers' and, in similar ways, from some of the '150 Hours Courses' is that it is difficult or nearly impossible to define a language within strictly fixed and circumscribed bounds. The increasingly detailed and organized character of different cultural and linguistic spheres turns them into *systems*, if not objectively, at least in the lived emotional and fantasmatic experience of those who come close to them. The characteristic of a system is that it *speaks in and for itself*, and derives its power internally. Furthermore, it is so circumscribed and defined down to the last detail that it seems cut off from any context or roots. In this sense its fantasmatic potential is enormous and inevitably leads to a clash with another entity which is posited as discrete, the *unconscious*.

All this becomes very clear in the pedagogic experience, if one pays attention to the relation that is established with the *object of study* and with the mediating figure of the teacher. The ways of engaging and clashing with the learning material are well known: the entrance can be smooth, without any obstacles, but such access to learning may, however, turn out to signal a lack of creative ability or personal commitment. Alternatively, tenacious 'resistance' can then turn into hostility, obtuseness in the context in question, combined with an ability for critical thought in other regards which, none the less, risks being lost and wasted. It seems that one can only enter a given system in a state of sleep and amnesia, or at any rate forgetful of oneself; the alternative is to remain outside and obstinately bang one's head against the wall, denying its existence.

In women's experience these events highlight issues clearly linked to emotional, affective, and sexual life. Often the woman prepares herself to take on a system of signs that she feels are alien to her, in an exceptional spirit of self-abnegation, discipline, and sacrifice. She is prepared to sacrifice part of herself to enter an order which she invests with value and authority, the forces of attraction. Alternatively she works out ways of 'resisting' that are double-edged, on the one hand claiming misfortune and powerlessness ('I don't know how to', 'I can't'), on the other omnipotence ('that's no use', 'that doesn't count', 'I know what I need to know'). The presence of the teacher as an intermediary in this process, whether a man or woman, who has consciously worked out the underlying motivations in his or her own cultural history, has a profound effect. The teacher who fails to focus on the relationship between culture and experience, emotional life and study in his or her own life, and sheds no light on the unconscious roots of all knowledge and theory, can only *expel* knowledge, simply reducing it to 'teaching material', and *expel* the difficulties encountered in transmitting it, simply reducing them to 'psycho-dynamics'. On the one hand, this brings reassurance and on the other an impoverishment of personal, expressive, and creative abilities.

If one manages to make the connections that every individual can trace in him or herself between a not absolutely 'unknown' unconscious and a series of given languages which are neither fixed for all time, nor as coherent as they seem, this makes for a free-flowing circulation of ideas and emotions. It then becomes possible to give a *historical* dimension to personal experience which builds up its force by being repressed and marginalized. On the other hand, it also becomes more possible to dent the absolutist pretensions of the cultural systems, which, like most human constructs, stem from confusion and complexity, and often disappear, because, like all theories, they are not separate from the realm of passions which become all the more potent, the less they are understood.

In a cultured person, one can take for granted that the learning effort has altered the equilibrium between the internal and external worlds, even if to differing effect. Like the transactions which induce modifications in an original order, so the entry of an individual into culture produces upheavals, conflicts, and psychological compromises. One can live with a permanent conflict between dream and reality, private and public, emotions and productive activity. Alternatively, one side of the polarity in this internal war can be hived off and rearranged in a separate sphere (the family, love, friendship). This leaves the other side freer to get on with a recognized activity. The inner world can end up diminished by years of discipline and social activity, or can live through its contradictory impulses of omnipotence that prevent the ordered development of work and intellectual production.

Behind the most obvious guises of 'deprivation', 'lack', and 'inability', the uneducated person often preserves an image of integrity and self-containment and cultivates an ideal of perfection and rapid progress that tends to impede learning. Going back to school is the sign of the 'offence' or 'wrong' which society has done to both men and women, but which weighs particularly heavily on women. ('Women weren't made to study or to do paid work.') However, behind the visible, historically inflicted wound, there is the expectation of redemption and *recompense*. It is fantasized not in terms of a slow process of learning but as a magical panacea, putting one's trust in hope rather than in one's own ability. ('I hope I can make it.')

In a '150 Hours Course' like the one at Affori which was attended in the main by women, and run by feminist women teachers who had experience of personal psychoanalysis or of analysis in the *gruppi dell'inconscio*, these problems became visible. They became visible not only for women, but for all those who have the patience and desire to analyse themselves and their activities.

PART II

Criticism:
theory/practice

9 Female identity and Italian cinema of the 1950s

GIOVANNA GRIGNAFFINI

Translated by Paul Monaco and Rosamund Howe

EDITORS' INTRODUCTION

As Giovanna Grignaffini explains at the beginning of her text, it is part of a work in progress on the vicissitudes of female identity being carried out at the Bologna Women's Research and Documentation Centre. The centre was set up in 1977 by women from various backgrounds – including the Women's Movement, the trade-union movement, and the university – in response to the need for a 'place' where women's intellectual life could find expression and where women's culture could be produced and exchanged. The various initiatives for research and documentation on women and the Women's Movement had the effect of adding to the archives, bibliographic materials, and research facilities which the centre already supplied. The link with the local area and its culture is an important aspect of the centre's research and documentation activities. Consequently it was decided that it should obtain recognition from the Bologna Municipality, which has been under left-wing control for many years and which now provides it with financial support and administrative personnel. The research launched at the centre included projects on women's condition, motherhood, and the Women's Movement in the Bologna region. The wide-ranging research on the vicissitudes of women's identity covered not only literature, the cinema, and history but also natural sciences and themes linked to the body and health. Its starting-point was the view that identity has many different time-scales, ranging from the short span of a biography to the *longue durée* of history and the apparently timeless field of biology.

Giovanna Grignaffini, who teaches history of cinema at Bologna University, initiated a research project on women and cinema with the publication of *Sequenza segreta* (1981), an anthology co-edited with Piera Detassis. The research has continued, in parallel and in conjunction with her work at the university, as an aspect of the centre's project on women's identity. She took charge of the cinema section. Her interest in psychoanalysis developed into an urgent need to rediscover and reappropriate the instruments of historical and sociological analysis.

The following thoughts and observations are drawn from the work achieved in the first stage of a larger project initiated by the Bologna Women's Research and Documentation Centre. This project on the vicissitudes of female identity draws on various different disciplines and methods of approach which all, however, work towards the same objective. Within this context we approach the Italian cinema of the 1950s (the central object of our investigation) with a particular point of view, that is we treat it as an apparatus with the capacity to function as 'operator' of female identity. This account must therefore be read, not like a polished essay, but, more problematically, as a work in progress, the principal object of which is to illustrate a project and its guidelines, to clarify and expose its main methodological premises.

I should consequently start by pointing out that my terms of reference and my place of enunciation are very far from an essentialist argument about 'female specificity' (understood as a basic category for a study of creativity, language, critical analysis, and film theory) but are located within the *history of cinema*.

This point ought not to be underestimated. The history of cinema (the cinematic institution and apparatus) has suffered from a repression as women have approached the question of cinema in recent years.

Why has this repression taken place? Firstly, there is a tactical reason, connected to the need to wipe out a historical exclusion by an exemplary gesture of symbolic reappropriation. This gesture had to be able to span the history of cinema, and follow up the clues which led the female subject to discover itself to be a central and privileged element in the organization of a discourse. From this perspective, analyses of the poetics of women's cinema and structural analyses of some genres of 'classical' cinema (especially the *film noir*) contribute to a similar degree.

Closely connected to this and even more deeply rooted in the way in which the relationship of woman and cinema is still played out today, there is a strategic reason which can explain why women have repressed the history of cinema. This is a response to the need to affirm 'the feminine' as an ideology, or rather as a theoretical ideology, and has concentrated on the study of those aspects of cinema that are relevant to, and reveal points of contact with, the theory of the subject. Both analytic study of individual works and more general attention to the theoretical discourses on the cinema can thus meet under the aegis of the privilege accorded to psychoanalysis as methodology.

Rather than discussing the individual results produced by each of these approaches, I would now like to consider the overall mechanism that directed and determined them. It is a mechanism which, having carved out privileged areas of reflection and analysis within the cinema, has finally transformed the institution into a 'good object' for a particular kind of female spectator – the analyst. Thus it is a symbolic gesture of reappropriation and of reconciliation, a gesture that does not question exclusion and difference but rather circumscribes them in fields which it can control. In my view, not even textual analysis, the most productive recent undertaking for women's criticism, can evade the logic of this destiny founding, as it does, its own specificity in relation to two key notions, that of *writing* and that of the *model female spectator*.

I would like to dwell briefly on this problem. Indeed, since the position occupied by textual analysis is the direct opposite of that occupied by the history of cinema, it may enable us to discover, antithetically, some of the premises on which our work on the 1950s should develop.

It seems to me that *textual analysis* applied to films can be defined as a method of *critical discourse*: a doubly perverse method. Critical discourse is mediated by writing and produces a double substitution of the object of desire. First of all, any critical operation has a founding gesture at its base: '*To pass from reading to criticism* means changing desire, no longer desiring the work, but its language' (Barthes 1966). Secondly there is a particular operation at the basis of every textual analysis of film: the alien word is condemned to find only mere simulacra, and fictitious paraphrases of an 'eternally unattainable text' (Bellour 1979).

To digress for a moment, we could ask ourselves why women have granted such pre-eminence to a kind of critical discourse in which the sense of loss and absence of the filmic text is concealed by a completeness and omnipotence in the writing. This writing is both assertive and emotionally detached, intending to annihilate itself completely in the object of its own desire at the very moment that it changes it into an irretrievable object, lost for ever. Is this not perhaps the most radical, subtle, and anodyne way of turning an alien, threatening body (the cinema) into an insubstantial shadow?

To return after this digression, it is indeed ambiguity about the notion of writing which allows us to place textual analysis in the field of critical discourse. Is it not simply a refinement that masks the author's presence? It seems apposite therefore to cite some of Foucault's observations defining the notion of writing as a way of transposing 'the empirical characteristics of an author to a transcendental anonymity' (Foucault 1979: 17). Foucault writes:

> In granting a primordial status to writing, do we not, in effect, simply reinscribe in transcendental terms the theological affirmation of its sacred origin or a critical belief in its creative nature? To say that writing, in terms of the particular history it made possible, is subjected to forgetfulness and repression, is this not to reintroduce in transcendental terms the religious principle of hidden meanings (which require interpretation) and the critical assumption of implicit significations . . . (which gives rise to commentary)?   (Foucault 1979: 17)

A hidden meaning: a need to interpret. An implicit signification: a need to comment. It is these two notions that place textual analysis back in the field of critical discourse. Even analyses which are most heavily weighted towards the pragmatic efficiency of the text finally lead back there. In this case, however, the movement comes from the exact opposite direction to the previous one. To paraphrase Foucault, we could say that the concept of the 'model reader' is a way of transposing the empirical character of the reader into a transcendental anonymity. 'The critic cannot take the place of the reader in any way', Barthes wrote (1966).

Not even, we might add, when the critic's writing appears to be a paraphrase of the literal meaning of the text. The universal and abstract character that the critic attributes to a hypothetical model reader is nothing but an effect of writing, a production not of the text under analysis, but of the language that aspires to describe it. Underlying this complex operation of mediation there remains merely the founding gesture from which every reading is born: *this is how it is, here and now, for me.* Can the notion of empirical author, like that of empirical reader, also lose its position as founding principle? And what would a history of cinema which took this loss as its starting-point be like? What kind of exposure could a discourse on 'the feminine' find within it?

Our work developed around these three questions. Foucault gave some practical guidelines in the essay already cited; for example, when he indicated the possibility of considering the author simply as a 'complex and variable function of discourse', when he confirmed the need to circumscribe 'the places and the functions that the disappearance of the author has made visible', and above all when he identified the possibility of thinking of historical research as a 'historical analysis of discourse'.

New questions, therefore, new possible fields of investigation:

> 'What are the modes of existence of this discourse?' 'Where does it come from; how is it circulated; who controls it?' 'What placements are determined for possible subjects?' 'Who can fulfil these diverse functions of the subject?'
>
> (Foucault 1979: 29)

Let us say, then, that our work is intended to develop along phenomenological lines, attempting to combine cinema, history, and history of cinema, and aiming at a historical analysis of discourse. To my mind, this perspective offers a number of advantages both on the level of film historiography and as regards the possibility of reintroducing into it the issue of 'the feminine', understood as a point of view from which to look at the history of cinema.

Traditional film historiography has predominantly tended to create a clear-cut separation between the economic, political, and the symbolic. On one side are the structures, the production, and the market; on the other, the authors, the works, the styles, the trends, the national cinemas or 'schools'. On the one hand, the sociology of the public, on the other, the systems of representation.

On the one hand, the ideology represented, on the other, the ideology of filmic writing. To speak instead of 'placements and modes' of the existence-production-circulation-appropriation of discourses, means breaking down the binary separation right at its root. Further, through the historical analysis of discourse we can bring back into play the four key notions which constitute the specificity of the cinema understood as a *medium*.

First there is the idea of chance understood as a discursive method closely related to the cinema's productive process.[1] Secondly, the notion of *intertextuality* conceived as a system of quotation that the cinema and more generally the media have introduced in the 'age of mechanical reproduction'. Finally, there are the notions of the cinematic apparatus and institution understood as places of production of discourse, able to determine the conditions of existence of each particular discourse.[2] Let us say then that our research has singled out as the object of its analysis the problem of *female identity*, as a discourse produced by a specific medium (the cinema), to be investigated within a precise historical period: after the Second World War in Italy.

The historical period is very brief, relatively arbitrary, and bounded by two epoch-making events: the end of the war and the beginning of the economic boom. It mainly consists of the 'grim gloomy 1950s' (as Pasolini called them); the representation of women during this period has been overshadowed by the positive models which came before and after: 'the Partisan woman' of the Resistance and the 'emancipated woman' of the 1960s.

Recent historiography of women, however, has started to look at those 'dark years' in a new light. If there can really only be a representation of some collective behaviour, there can nevertheless be a logic made up of 'secret and individual steps' (Stella 1980), steps which were still being taken within the ambit of the family, but where women were now less protected, due to a process that the cinema perhaps helped to set in motion.

Then two further premises are necessary to describe the work. To speak of female identity means not only to speak of social models and stereotypes of identity put into circulation by a historical era, but also of those processes and mechanisms that a historical era has primed, promoted, and authorized: in other words, made *possible*. As the cinema is the main object of our study, it is clear that the category used most frequently will be that of the *visible*, in the meaning defined by Pierre Sorlin as 'what appears that can be photographed and represented on the screen in a certain era' (1977: 68).

It should also be remembered, however, that the discourse produced by the cinema goes beyond this, and has to do with the whole range of behaviours and models for the subject that the cinematic institution sets up. Thus in studying the cinema of the 1950s, we intend to trace not only the features of its history, but also the features which made that history possible.

Moving to specific elements of analysis, I want to emphasize, first of all, a point I have already made about the cinematic apparatus. This issue must be treated rather differently when viewed from a historical perspective instead of from a strictly theoretical point of view.

Indeed, once female identity is posed as the central object of discourse, it becomes fundamentally important to highlight the overdetermining role which the apparatus exercises on the cinema's processes of identification. It is essential to review Baudry's (1976) and Metz's (1977) theories of homology between the apparatus and the mirror stage, of the spectator as 'all-perceiving', of the distinction between 'primary identification and secondary identification in the cinema', and so on. It is equally essential to go back over Barthes's (1979) analyses of 'going to the cinema', which he regards as a place for the *flâneur*, the site of urban 'quest', and a means by which the subject can lose itself isolated in the womb-like and regressive darkness of the auditorium.

These issues have to be dialectically integrated with others; that is, on the one hand, the wider historical context and, on the other, the specificity of the subjects under analysis; our attention can thus shift away from a discourse on the female spectator regarded as a synthesis of abstract and concrete functions, a dialectical union of 'model' and 'empirical' female spectators.

When, where, and how did women go to the cinema in Italy in the 1950s? Did the screen really offer separation and isolation? And was the darkness of the auditorium really so womb-like?

Let us look at some facts. In Italy in the early 1950s there were about 8,000 cinemas, evenly distributed throughout the country, and not only concentrated in the big cities, as happened much later. Moreover, the real mainstay of the film industry was re-release cinemas located mainly in villages and country areas. Of the 8,000 cinemas only half conform to the classical definition of the term, while the other half were part of multi-purpose facilities (run mainly by clubs, cultural associations, political parties, etc.), dominated by the village circuit which alone numbered up to 2,000 halls (Quaglietti 1980). Programming was mainly based on the single feature with rigid differentiation between weekday evenings and holidays. Going to the cinema was predominantly a group habit and for women (and particularly for teenage girls), it was the most popular permissible means of getting out of the house. Then the cinema (with the bar, games room, etc., its inevitable ramifications) was the centre of social life, the place to be seen in public, to meet members of the opposite sex, and where different generations mixed. Even the ritual of actually watching the film deviates surprisingly from the theoretical model of spectatorship. Due both to the arrangement of halls and constant interruptions in the flow of images as the audience continually moved about and changed places in the rituals of communication that took place during screening, viewing was subject to a series of intrusions and interferences by the real world that made distraction a significant part of the experience of going to the cinema and rather similar to watching television. It is no coincidence that Italy's first television sets were located in public places: cafés, clubs, halls. So not even where television watching is concerned is it possible to make abstract generalizations about being 'imprisoned in the family' and the domestic sphere, since 'going to watch television', like 'going to the movies', was a public experience, an occasion for socializing and getting out of the house.

Film spectatorship, then, in rural Italy in the 1950s went beyond the question of cinema itself. It was a largely social event with a specific significance of its own for the question of identity, going beyond the significance of the actual film. Nor should we forget the part played by 'coming attractions': posters and stickers put up in front of cinemas and other places where people meet. These were real forms of previewing, an induction into the images of the film, or even, for very many people, their only actual experience of the cinema (Brunetta 1983).

The second point which should be emphasized concerns the prevalent models for women's representation. These models were produced by the cinema, certainly, but were also part of a system of references, quotations, emphases, extensions, that built up a multi-media intertextuality through the use of media different from, but compatible with, the cinema (especially photoromances and photographs). In particular glossy magazines like *Grand Hotel* (1946), *Bolero* (1947) and the most famous, *Novella Film* (1948, with a readership of 2 million, almost exclusively female) used the cinema not only as a formal reference structure (photographs in sequence with captions and strip cartoons); even more significantly, they used the cinema as an element of attraction and induction into the stories and characters portrayed. Due to the much weaker projective power of magazines compared to the cinema, a film's story and a star's body, once transposed from one medium to the other, lost the divine 'aura' that the cinema gave them, lost their mythic quality, and became part of daily life. Once these stories and bodies circulated in daily life, they acquired a determining influence on the 'sentimental education' (understood to mean a person's relationship both with the self and with the other) of an entire generation. They establish the main terms around which the visible of the 1950s revolves. The mass availability of photography was, however, also undoubtedly of central importance.

In Italy in the 1950s two particular kinds of photograph became popular, the *family photo* and the *portrait photo* (they had already become popular in other countries, especially France and the USA, during the 1930s). We shall consider two relevant comments that are only apparently antithetical, since both attempt to define a situation in transformation in which traces of the past are overlaid with the new. So, on the one hand, as Susan Sontag observes: 'Photography becomes a rite of family life just when . . . the very institution of the family starts undergoing radical surgery' (1977: 8). The family photograph becomes a kind of catalogue or dictionary of lost experience, a way of restating the unity of the family just as it was beginning to show signs of falling apart. On the other hand, there is the portrait photograph – 'see[ing] oneself differently from in a mirror' (Barthes 1984: 12) – which produced an important revolution in identity mechanisms and processes.

Roland Barthes writes: 'The photograph is the advent of myself as other: a cunning dissociation of consciousness from identity' (Barthes 1984: 12). Not only, therefore, does photography designate a new possible field of historical research (what Barthes defines as the 'History of Looking'), it also constitutes one of the privileged places through which the visible is produced in a historical era. Indeed, there can only be a photograph of what has already reached the status of an event in the ideological-cultural plane, and each historical era sees only what has been affirmed on the social scene: 'There can be no evidence, photographic or otherwise, of an event until the event itself has been named and characterized' (Sontag 1977: 19).

What about cinema? Cinema constitutes the secret model for those posed bodies in portrait photographs, whose right of entry into the territory of the visible had been decreed by the cinematic institution itself, in its attempt to make a clear-cut separation from Fascist cinema's portrayal of the female body.

Finally we come to my last point, one that serves as a general background to the others I have dealt with. Why is Italian cinema of the 1950s permeated to such an obsessive degree by the female body and eroticism? What are the rules governing the creation of a female star in a cinema which is still largely subject to neorealist tendencies?

From the point of view of the market, Italian neorealism as a school was undoubtedly marginal and avant-garde. Analysed, however, from the point of view of the cinematic institution, it had the essential function of providing a moment of theoretical-ideological legitimation of what was produced during the 1950s. Texts relevant to our topic lie at the heart of neorealism: these include various writings by Antonioni, De Santis, and Visconti, which appeared in the early 1940s in the magazine *Cinema* ('Per un film sul fiume Po', 'Per un paesaggio italiano', 'Il linguaggio del rapporti', and 'Cinema antropomorfico'); also a film by De Santis: *Bitter Rice* (1949) is unanimously regarded as making the transition between the neorealist experiment and the popular cinema of the 1950s. It is no coincidence that this was the first Italian post-war film to win international acclaim. It made Silvana Mangano a star, it opened the way to stardom for various younger pin-ups like Sofia Loren and Gina Lollobrigida, and it established a kind of drama that was half-way between melodrama and the pulp novel. Foucault's notion of the *transdiscursive* can be usefully applied to the neorealist texts, texts that 'produce[d] . . . the possibility and the rules of formation of other texts', texts which are 'initiators of discursive practices', able to produce a discourse and its rules (Foucault 1979: 24).

Let us examine them briefly. As far as the above texts are

concerned, it must be emphasized that the tension running through them relates entirely to the problem of the rebirth of the Italian cinema, a process which relied on the 'rediscovery' of two complementary centralities: landscape and the human presence in it. These are complementary centralities, and the most original aspects of these texts lie in the attempt to define this complementarity (Grignaffini 1982). There are two points worth mentioning: the relationship between human beings and landscape and the 'reciprocal and constant interchange of signs and reflections between the two'. What does this mean in practice?

It means that, just as the landscape bears the signs of human activity inscribed on it affecting its form and development, so people bear the signs of the landscape in which they live on their faces and bodies and in their actions. And although 'landscape' should not be understood in a purely literal sense, this exchange of signs and reflections takes place mainly in the visible. To put it another way, human beings are represented as *operators* of the landscape, in the sense that they both receive and regulate its modulations, the geographical as well as the anthropological; human beings and the landscape are then, in turn, represented as *operators* of a new national identity and physical characteristics, bodies, and gestures, restored to an immediately legible *transparency*, also become landscape.

In short, on the one hand the principle of 'the exposition of reality', the aesthetic foundation of neorealism, was applied to the actor: De Santis discussed the 'authenticity of actors' gestures' and Visconti the 'instinctive language of actors'. On the other hand a new typical Italian could be found through the use of people who were most integrated with the landscape, nearest to the earth, and most ready to move in harmony with nature. And a film like *Bitter Rice*, and more generally the cinema of the 1950s, refers precisely to a femininity understood as *naturalness*, body 'of the earth', in harmony with the landscape.

Other evidence on the question of the 'new archetypal Italian' can also be found. For example, the 'language of relationships': this meant gradual progress towards the Pudovkinian 'type', emphasizing, however, solely the question of *typical* natural physical characteristics. This had the final effect of diminishing the importance of actors' interpretative skill, which moved to another level in consequence. The 'new' professional skill of the neorealist actor essentially meant the need to keep to his or her own nature: firstly, on the figurative plane, then on the attitudinal and behavioural plane. The actor and the character have to meet and blend into each other. This happens not only through naturalism in performance but also through the actor becoming the character he or she is portraying, starting from the premise that a face and a body can tell a story, demonstrate what led up to it, and show what happens next, with the consequences indelibly fixed on them. Ultimately, neorealist treatment of actors turns out to be quite simple: new actors were trained and film actors of the 1930s were retrained, on the basis of the assumption that *face and body are language*.

Within this assumption, 'real' life was used as a new source for the recruitment of actors (the aesthetic of the 'actor taken off the street') *and* at the same time actors were brought in from the theatre (Anna Magnani is a good example).

It is not therefore altogether true to say that the effect of neorealism was to 'de-theatricalize' actors' performances. This is both because 'naturalization of performance' is based on a very solid theatrical tradition, Stanislavsky's experiment which was transposed to the cinema through Lee Strasberg, and also because the traditions of theatre should be approached in a different way and with a different focus on its conventions.

Neorealism generally favoured naturalism in representation and tried to introduce the same principle into performance. And the real innovation of neorealism was to re-establish a balance between representation and performance (a balance that was much more precarious in the Italian cinema of the 1930s).

But the analysis can be taken even further, since the theory of the 'physical type' shatters the principle of interchangeability of roles and faces, of the ability to *become* without *being*, the ability to act a surface appearance without the inner essence that goes with it. Are these not perhaps the factors that gave rise to the creation of stars? These factors include constant confusion between actor and character, physical presence and role. Nor should it be forgotten that the *aesthetics of transparency*, with all its connotations of verisimilitude, is the most appropriate language for nourishing the real and imaginary life of the star.

Leaving aside the moral, sociological, and production aspects, it is clear that with neorealism the Italian film industry prepared to usher in the star system, though some important changes and modifications were yet to come. Indeed, a cinema with spatial and temporal continuity, based on location shooting, the figure in the landscape, long takes, and rejection of close-ups, could only shift attention from the *face* to the *body*, from facial expression to the dynamics of gesture.

This does much to explain why a large element in neorealism was interested in popular theatre, notably variety shows and supporting programmes. These became the preferred source for the recruitment of actors in post-war neorealist cinema. In these kinds of theatre, *total use of the body* is the instrument and form of communication, rather than interpretative, psychological, or dramatic refinements. The same form of communication is used even more explicitly, and with no recourse to artifice, in beauty contests. It is no accident that the foremost exponents of neorealism – Visconti, Zavattini, De Sica, De Santis – all presided on the juries of Miss Italy contests from 1946 on. It is no accident that the Italian stars of the 1950s – Silvana Mangano, Lucia Bosé, Sofia Loren, Gina Lollobrigida, Silvana Pampanini, etc. – were discovered in these beauty contests where the rite of 'Italianness', now expressed in physical forms and movements, could be celebrated to the full.

The cinematic institution found a new *visible* to satisfy to the full its need for revitalization and redemption (on the ideological, production, and symbolic levels): the female body, intact and uncontaminated by the look of Fascist ideology, a creature of the earth, rich with joyous sensuality, generous in its proportions, warm, and familiar: a body-landscape, along whose outline you could read the future of a nation that had to start again from scratch.

I will conclude with a question: whatever the reasons for its appearance, did the particular image of the Italian female body in the 1950s, inextricably linked to a cinematic style, work as a 'mirror stage' for the female spectators of the time?

NOTES

1   See Burch (1973).
2   See Metz (1977) and Baudry (1976).

10 *The accessibility of the text: an analysis of* The Lady from Shanghai

LUCILLA ALBANO

Translated by Letizia Ciotti Miller

EDITORS' INTRODUCTION

The following text is an analysis of Orson Welles's *The Lady from Shanghai*. Written by Lucilla Albano, who teaches history of cinema at the University of Florence, it documents what was really an essential stage in women's – and men's – 'scientific' research into cinema in Italy and elsewhere. This important phase was textual analysis. The methodology proposed by Lucilla Albano for approaching the text is still little known or explored and is fertile in possibilities. It is derived from the theory of Ignacio Matte Blanco, a psychoanalist now living in Rome. His theoretical discourse is founded on an interest in mathematics, in particular the theory of logical types and the concept of the infinite. Taking the characteristics of the unconscious described by Freud and rereading them in terms of mathematical logic, Matte Blanco identifies the existence in the unconscious of the principle of symmetry, a principle by which a relation and its converse are treated as identical. Matte Blanco then puts forward the theory of bi-logic, the result of two types of logic: the bivalent (that is, based on the Aristotelian pattern) and the symmetrical, which subverts the principle of incompatibility. Matte Blanco's psychoanalytic theory does not conform to the Freudian-Lacanian reference system which is predominant in psychoanalytically based Anglo-American film studies. It can offer a new, interesting research prospect which takes among its starting-points the affirmation of contradiction, multiple times and spaces, 'infinite' experiences. Matte Blanco's seminal text is *The Unconscious as Infinite Sets* (1975). Amongst others are 'Expression in symbolic logic of the characteristics of the system ucs' (1959) and his writings on artistic creation which were recently published in the Italian magazine *Filmcritica* (1986).

The Lady from Shanghai (1947) is a long flashback. Dominated by the voice-off and voice-over of its protagonist-narrator, it is the story of something that happened a long time ago, the story of an experience which the narrator, by *verbalizing* it, recollects, reformulates, and explains. As he puts it into words, he can interpret it, as a dreamer does, telling a dream. In the same way, Welles replaces a dream-like vision with a cinematic one whose material is the 'stuff that dreams are made of'.

By the same token, the tale could be compared to childhood memories, and be a *re-evocation*. This is partly because of what the narrator says at the end of the film: 'The only way to stay out of trouble is to grow old. So I guess I'll concentrate on that. Maybe I'll live so long that I'll forget her. Maybe I'll die trying.' Words which shift the story back to the narrator's youth. The story can also be related to Freud's ideas on childhood memories, that they are a mixture of truth and falsehood in which it is difficult to find our way. All this arouses a sense of displacement and inaccessibility in the spectator, who also experiences some difficulty in following the plot, even though there is nothing in it which cannot be explained, and 'everything makes sense'. We could also make a connection here with our perceptions when we are half-asleep and half-awake, when we day-dream , when our senses grow drowsy. It is like the sensation of falling, as the hero does when he slides down the long chute in the Amusement Park, a state of loss of self typical of day-dreaming.

The story of *The Lady from Shanghai* belongs in a certain sense to all of these different forms of story-telling. It could be a dream, a childhood memory, or a day-dream, or perhaps all of them at once – there is no way of knowing. Dream-like, fantastic, and evocative, it is the story of a formative experience which 'transforms' – as the sailor O'Hara, in fact, is transformed by the end of the story.

The flashback structure of the film is only established through the sound-track and through the voice-off of Michael O'Hara-Orson Welles. His narrative 'presence' has a double function. On the one hand, his is the voice of the story-teller and has an objective position in relation to the subjective nature of everything the sailor O'Hara lives and experiences. On the other hand, it is also the voice of the artist 'creator', the 'mythic hero' who talks about his adventures, and who has transfigured 'his phantasies into truths of a new kind which are valued by men as precious reflections of reality' (Freud 1973: XII, 224). That is, the narrator's voice places itself subjectively in relation to the objectivity of the film's protagonist, Michael O'Hara. This constant oscillation between subjectivity and objectivity creates a dialectic which suspends the story between fantasy and reality – between being complete fantasy on the part of the story-teller and a description of actual events.

The plot may be the first guideline to a reading of the work because it locates the film in the *noir* and melodrama genres (although in its own original way), and represents an overlap between the two. Interpreting *The Lady from Shanghai* in these terms, however, means giving only a partial reading of the film. But a reading in terms of genre, *noir* and melodrama, does allow us to consider the relationship between the characters in terms of the Oedipal triangle.

Thus Elsa Bannister (Rita Hayworth) can be assigned the role of the mother whom the young hero Michael O'Hara seeks to conquer and carry away from the rich and corrupt father, Arthur Bannister (Everett Sloane). This interpretation, to my mind, offers the greatest insight into the extraordinary narrative and visual wealth of the film, relating not only to its treatment of the content of the unconscious (in this case, the Oedipus complex) but also to its treatment of the forms or, rather, the laws, which govern the language of the unconscious. These laws were first identified by Freud and have more recently been defined by Matte Blanco in *The Unconscious as Infinite Sets* (1975).[1] The suggestions in Matte Blanco's book provided me with a specific theoretical grid for an analysis of the 'infinite' text, *The Lady from Shanghai*.

The central assumption of my analysis is that Welles's film functions on a *system of differences* which are simultaneously presented and eliminated, so as to create with them and in their place a *system of identities*.

The experience of the sailor hero, Michael O'Hara, is dominated by a single emotional element which pervades the script:
the feeling of living in a nightmare of pain and anxiety caused by
an unacceptable desire. O'Hara's position as a puritan hero, as a
man of principle, who fights and condemns corruption and
immorality, is subjugated and undermined by the lure of the
'monsters', the 'sharks' (Bannister and Grisby), whom he
struggles against. And to add to the anxiety, the main representative of this 'monstrosity' is a beautiful and fascinating woman,
spectacular, in a position of bondage and vulnerability, a sensual
woman, who is 'in love' with the hero – Elsa Bannister-Rita
Hayworth.

What Welles seems to say here is the opposite of what he
leaves unsaid but implies, because 'the repressed person who
frees himself tries to gain satisfaction by protecting himself with
an ideological motivation' (Wittels 1962). Welles is actually aiming his darts at the puritanism, moralism, and bigotry of American society which O'Hara champions in the film. He does this by
presenting evil characters who are opposed to the hero but to
whom the hero, at the same time, becomes assimilated. [2] Michael's
anguish therefore derives from his inability to differentiate himself from the Bannisters (while the narrator's voice-off is precisely that of one who has escaped from the nightmare and who
can differentiate himself) and from his being like and, at the same
time, unlike the Bannisters; and like and, at the same time,
unlike Elsa.

The sailor Michael O'Hara is a poor, honest, and moralistic
idealist, and the Bannisters are corrupt, cruel, and immoral mil-
lionaires. But Michael too will be corrupted by money, and act in
immoral ways. Michael does not want to see Elsa any more
because she is married to someone else, but at the same time he
desires her, and asks her to run away with him. His whole being
is attracted to Elsa, but at the same time he detests her. 'Why
should anyone want to live around us?' Elsa asks her husband.
She is at the same time splendid and horrible, like the places they
visit together – Acapulco or the sumptuous, swanky, but horrible
picnic where no one has a good time ('I've never seen anything
worse,' Michael tells Bannister). This world of polarizations and
attractions originates from primary, absolute elements. Michael
is a man and Elsa is a woman. This is the main polarization but it
is also obviously the main attraction. Michael is strong, Elsa is

beautiful (Bannister says on the evening of the picnic: 'He's strong, she's beautiful') and therefore dangerous. The man is attracted to the beautiful womàn but at the same time he is afraid of being weakened by her.

From these primary elements, we come to the secondary, cultural elements: Michael comes from the west and Elsa from the east, but the place where they meet is New York, in the west, but on the East Coast, thus in the east in relation to the West Coast. Michael is poor and Elsa is rich, but Elsa will be poor if she leaves her husband, and Michael will have $5,000 after he concludes his shady deal with Grisby. Elsa is heading towards Evil, while Michael wants to go towards Good, but he will be accused of a murder and found guilty. Everything in the film – the dialogue, the characters, the settings, the images, the editing, the way the scenes are shot, the entire production – combines to convey the sense in which truths and lies, affirmations and negations, reality and fiction, attraction and repulsion, differences and identities, coexist and cohabit in the same characters, the same places. We shall see how this is achieved.

DIALOGUE AND CHARACTERS

The characters are like interlocking shapes in a jigsaw or pieces in a chess game where each is a pawn in the strategy of the other, and where everyone tries to appear to be something they are not, while claiming that they are not what they appear to be. Furthermore, the dialogue is utterly inconsistent because it develops as if the principle of contradiction did not exist. Things are stated only to be negated later on: what is stated means something and at the same time means its own opposite. 'I am not what you think I am, I just try to be like that,' Elsa tells Michael. In reality, Elsa is exactly what she appears to be – she remains with her husband purely out of self-interest, she is a 'man-eater', a deceiving woman, capable of lying and killing for the sake of money. At the same time, she wants to appear as something she is not.

Michael maintains that he is not a hero, even though he appears to be one when he rescues Elsa from an attack ('I start out in this story a bit like a hero, which I most certainly am not'). But he will behave like a 'hero' when he finds a way of escaping from the courtroom, discovering the real culprit, and saving himself in the end from the woman who wanted to cheat him and lead him down the road to ruin. Michael is honest and innocent, but he agrees to 'kill' a man for money, even though the murder is only simulated. He does not kill Grisby, but he signs a confession saying that he did. Grisby wants people to think he is 'dead' while he is really alive, but later on he really dies, murdered by Elsa. Bannister wants to appear cynical, sure of himself, but he will lose a case for the first time in his career just to make sure that he does not lose his wife. He does not want to lose his wife, but it is he who kills her in the end, emptying a whole magazine of ammunition into her. In the Amusement Park's Magic Mirror Maze, with their guns pointed at one another, Bannister says to Elsa 'killing you is killing myself'.

Finally, in the penultimate scene of the film, the dying Elsa says to Michael, 'You can fight but what good is it?' 'You mean we can't win?' Michael asks her. And Elsa replies, 'No, we can't win.' With this negation, she cancels out the sense of her preceding sentence. This is essentially what happens in all the dialogue I have quoted so far. The operation of the system of causality and the determination of meaning is constantly made dysfunctional by a series of statements which immediately become negations.

All of the characters are presented and represented according to figures and tropes. For example, Bannister is introduced through the image of his crutches. The crutches come first, and then Bannister, as if the body were a part of the crutches – that is, 'what is a proper part is treated as if it were improper.'[3] Bannister is therefore characterized as crippled, maimed, impotent – like a man who cannot keep his wife; and this is, after all, his position in the Oedipal triangle. Bannister always needs crutches, 'rhetorical prostheses', even in his conversation where his *hidden implications*, and his antiphrases, his ironies and metaphors ('According to George here, Michael is anxious to quit', 'Mr Grisby has just told me something that I'm very sorry to hear', '[Michael] makes a good bodyguard for you') declare the game of masculine rivalry for the possession of Elsa. This game is clearly revealed by Bannister (by now the betrayed and jealous husband, no longer the great lawyer) to Michael O'Hara (by now the wife's lover, no longer the lawyer's client in need of defence) only at the moment when the jury is about to re-enter the courtroom and pass a verdict of guilty on Michael.

It is Bannister who is assigned the film's most paradoxical yet most explicit moment in this multiplicity of identities and games of appearances. This is the scene in which Bannister is questioned as a witness for the prosecution and then cross-examines himself, playing two roles simultaneously, that of witness and that of defence lawyer.[4]

Grisby is often shot in close-up and full-face. His face and features are enlarged by the movie camera's 18-mm lens. He looks through a spyglass to see better, to bring things closer to him, and possess them with his ravenous gaze. The first time his close-up appears, it is juxtaposed with a point-of-view shot, through his spyglass, of Elsa in a bathing suit, her stupendous body revealed. That is, Grisby is curious and morbid, he desires Elsa and will do anything to possess her, plotting to kill his partner who is none other than Elsa's husband. But he will not succeed in having her either. On the contrary, he will be killed by Elsa, just as she will be killed by her husband. His position in the Oedipal triangle is to represent Bannister's double, his other.

Michael is almost always shown in half-light, from the back, or in profile. His face eludes the camera, just as in a dream the dreamer is an uncertain presence, whose body is not easily located or identifiable. Michael is like blotting paper, identifying with the other characters, but above all with Elsa. This impression is intensified not only by the fact that in the first part of the film, Elsa is always seen swimming or lying down – horizontal as it were – but also because she is privileged by the camera and lighting. If Michael is in half-light, she is in full light and radiant; and if Michael is shown in profile, she is shot full-face. Her body, just a year before, belonged to *Gilda*, who was, in the last resort, innocent. And so, in the play between appearance and reality, which belongs to both films, the song 'Amado mio' not only reminds us that Rita is Gilda but also that Gilda's body has been transformed into Elsa's and is thus, in the last resort, guilty.

MISE EN SCÈNE

This dream has the whole world as its setting. It is told as a fantastic and impossible journey where the Old World and the New World, west and east, north and south, come together. The voyage is both fantastic and real, and the different worlds converge in a single event and, at the end, a single place. No subsequent development is possible.[5]

Michael O'Hara has a 'mythic' past. He was born in Ireland, in the Old Continent, he fought for freedom in Spain, he has been to the coast of Brazil where he saw sharks devouring one another, and he has been in the jails of Australia. As a sailor, he has visited many countries, maybe every country in the world.[6]

Freud gives two examples in two different works which refer to an identical situation ('travelling' and 'moving to another country') and although they provide the same explanation of the workings of the unconscious, they are actually to do with opposite behaviours. In the first example, Freud writes, 'one is bound to employ the currency that is in use in the country one is exploring' (Freud 1973: XII, 225) and in the second, 'invading conquerors govern a conquered country not according to the judicial system which they find in force there, but according to their own' (Freud 1973: XXIII, 167). And, just as in Freud, two opposite examples have to do with the same process, that of the unconscious, so the sailor O'Hara behaves in opposite ways at one and the same time. He is an explorer who uses Bannister's currency in the role of the character O'Hara, and in his function as narrator he is a *conqueror* who acts in accordance with his own laws. O'Hara thus reveals, in his emotion which unifies the two behaviours and is conveyed to the spectator, an eruption of a logic of the unconscious, or rather a bi-logic, as Matte Blanco would say.[7]

But let us travel on with the sailor O'Hara, who, one night in New York, in Central Park, meets a beautiful girl, Elsa Bannister. Elsa tells him that she comes from a family of White Russians, that is from northern Europe, that she was born on the Chinese coast, at Chefoo, where Michael has also been. 'The second wickedest city in the world', Michael says. She has gambled in both Macao and Shanghai, even though 'you need more than luck in Shanghai', says Elsa, who gambles throughout the film in a game in which she would need much more than luck to win.

At the end of their encounter in Central Park, Elsa suggests to Michael that they take a pleasure trip to the 'west' (implying that New York is east) passing through the Caribbean, Mexico, and Acapulco, the south in relation to New York which is north. At the end of the cruise, Michael and Elsa land at San Francisco, in the west, where they also find the east, Chinatown, the land of the sunrise, and finally the Amusement Park, the Crazy House, and the Magic Mirror Maze. This itinerary takes them not only from east to west and at the same time vice versa, but also from the rational to the irrational, that is from reality (the trial) to theatre (Chinatown and the Chinese Theatre), to the state between sleep and wakefulness, then to sleep and dreams (the Amusement Park). And it also takes them from the site of the comprehensible to the incomprehensible, that is from legal proceedings to a theatrical performance in Chinese.

Unlikely as it may seem, each site is of equal value.[8] In fact, the trial functions as theatre: a farce is put on, the public awaits the entrance of the prima donna, Elsa Bannister, and follows the story of the crime as if a love triangle were being staged. The presence of the public impinges on the trial: the people in the public gallery and on the jury are enjoying themselves; they laugh at the legal proceedings which are constantly disrupted, at the lawyer's sophistry, and the judge's reprimands. At the end of the cross-examinations, nothing has been discovered except meaningless things that we already know. But the real theatre in Chinatown, on the other hand, is like a trial: the murder weapon is discovered, we find out who the murderer is, and Michael, instead of managing to escape as he did during the trial, is 'arrested', so to speak, not by the police who are looking for him in vain, but by Elsa's Chinese butler.

Finally, the site of irrationality, that of amusement and pleasure, and also sleep, sensory loss, and dreams, becomes a realm of rationality and law, where Michael is 'imprisoned' and the guilty are tragically punished. It is also like a theatre: the Crazy House is the fantastic setting, the entrance of Elsa's husband is the *coup de théâtre*, and the duel at the end is presented as phantasmagoria.

EDITING

While the system of causality is carried through, but also made inoperative, by the dialogue, the film's images represent the interior world, the most intimate feelings and desires of the protagonist, that is the 'dreamer' or 'child'. And they 'tell the story' of something else, supplementing, contradicting, anticipating, or disclosing undeclared thoughts and desires. In other words, the images are supported by the logic of the emotions.

Both the love story and the crime story are set in motion by two objects which Michael gives (the cigarette) or gives back (the gun) to Elsa, and both of them come from inside her bag.[9] It is Elsa, who sings 'Please don't kiss me', who first seeks the kisses of the sailor. After Michael violently refuses to kiss her, Elsa takes out a cigarette (perhaps the one that Michael gave her at their first meeting and that she had carefully wrapped in a white handkerchief inside her purse?) puts it in her mouth, and lights it; and it is then that Michael kisses her.

It is, again, visually, by means of a cigarette, that a secret bond is foreshadowed, the bond of love and crime between Elsa and Grisby, a bond that can only be consummated if Michael co-operates in the shady deal Grisby proposes to him. Elsa gives Grisby a cigarette to light for her, but *Michael* lights it, and then, in a close-up, we see Grisby's hand putting the 'lit' cigarette into Elsa's hand.

Elsa's gun is in the handbag abandoned in the park, which first attracts Michael's attention. It is Elsa's gun which is used in the crime Michael is accused of, which then proves to Michael that Elsa is the real culprit. Finally, it is Elsa's gun that is used in the double murder at the end.

Furthermore, Michael O'Hara's dealings with Elsa, as shown in the images, consist of a series of displaced, interrupted, or unsuccessful actions. Only once are they not interrupted (except, that is, by the cinematic process, by one image dissolving into the next; but the dissolve indicates not an interruption but a continuation, even if off-screen): this is the moment depicted by the final image in a series of shots which perfectly synthesize the relationship between Michael and Elsa, a relationship in which Michael's behaviour towards Elsa is dictated by incompatible emotions, emotions which are also those of the child for the mother (the *noir* Oedipus story). Matte Blanco has written:

Frequently the emotions are, in the logic of everyday life, incompatible with one another. The patient may wish, for instance, to destroy a mother image through tearing activities and simultaneously by poisonous attacks which paralyse her; or he may, in fantasy, make her explode or burn her, dissolve her and annihilate her so that nothing remains of the victim. But he may wish *at the same time* to preserve the most tender love-relationship with the image, to be united with her in such an intimate manner that they become one sole person, with a complete and total sharing of their being.

(Matte Blanco 1975: 205)

This dual and contrasting emotion is condensed in images of intense visual figuration and formal inventiveness in one of the film's most beautiful sequences, the one shot in the Steinhardt Aquarium in San Francisco. Of this sequence, Welles stated 'The screenplay was so boring that I said to myself, here we need something beautiful to look at.' The dialogue is of little importance and the sequence is a pretext for images of great visual power which subliminally enrich the meaning. As the two protagonists walk and speak, their entrances and exits are perfectly co-ordinated with tracking shots progressing from the medium shot, to medium close-up, close-up, and then extreme close-up, in front of enormous illuminated tanks containing different kinds of fish. In the final images of this sequence, when Michael and Elsa are framed in front of glass (and therefore, no longer in the 'real aquarium' but in a studio) the fish are distorted and enlarged in a special effect in which the small fish are made to look the same size as the big fish: beyond the film's trick photography, the small fish are *identical* to the big fish, and therefore to sharks, [10] those famous sharks Michael had seen devouring each other, to which he compared the Bannisters and Grisby. [11]

The shots of Elsa and Michael move progressively into close-up, framed more and more against the light, until their faces, in profile, and extreme close-up, are dark, illuminated by perfect back lighting, while it is the aquarium tanks and thus the devouring fish that are brightly lit. The two silhouettes blend into one, finally uniting in a kiss, which makes them a single and undefined whole, one and the same person, no longer differentiated. Behind the two lovers, the aquarium looms, with the sharks, who tear each other to pieces and devour each other, as if Michael were devouring Elsa (and Elsa were devouring Michael).

In the most famous and just as extraordinarily figurative final scene in the Amusement Park, with the Magic Mirror Maze, two contrasting emotions are represented through the fantastic and dream-like *mise-en-scène*. The emotions are *fear* of being destroyed, devoured, as when Michael, before being found by Elsa, slips and falls inside the giant devouring jaws of the Crazy House, and, immediately after, *desire* to destroy when, in the

maze of mirrors, he watches, standing aside and in the background, as Elsa's (and Bannister's) many faces are literally blown
to pieces, shot by shot. Reflection, multiplication, and fragment-
ation are used to indicate that what is happening is not simply a
showdown, the elimination of the guilty, but more importantly,
the destruction and annihilation of Michael's phantasms, his
projected identifications.

FINAL OBSERVATIONS ON CAMERA WORK

The Lady from Shanghai transgresses its genre not so much in the
fabula as in the narrative process or cinematic style, that is in its
'writing'. In fact, classical American genre cinema inclines towards
a dramaturgy in which everything, from the psychology of the characters, to the *mise-en-scène* and the *action*, is determined by the
narrative pace. There is no wasted action, time, or space.

Welles's camera has superlatively expressive freedom and
indicates that he is looking for camera positions and movements
which are aesthetic rather than functional. On the one hand, *The
Lady from Shanghai* imposes constant awareness of style using
unexpected framing and shots which continually show anomalous points of view or angles; these new, anomalous positions
are imposed by the camera's point of view. And on the other
hand, there is the use of depth-of-field (and the most wonderful
dream-like image of depth-of-field is that in which Elsa, dressed
in white, crosses a small street in Acapulco at night, while the
brightly lit city is stretched out at her feet); this depth-of-field
allows great freedom for the spectator's point of view. This is the
point of view that, as Bazin (1972) has described:

> takes in with equal sharpness the whole field of vision con-
> tained simultaneously within the dramatic field. It is no longer
> the editing that reflects what we see, thus giving it an a priori
> *significance*, it is the mind of the spectator that is forced to dis-
> cern, as in a sort of parallelepiped of reality with the screen as
> its cross section, the dramatic spectrum proper to the scene.
>
> (Bazin 1972: II, 28)

Thus a dominating system of constructed and fictional shots
coexists with the freedom and continuum of depth-of-field (the
'restitution of reality').

This text, for many reasons, is often regarded as obscure, ambiguous, confused, and fragmented, or, looked at in the best light, 'inaccessible'. [12] But, as I have shown, a unified reading is founded on the assumption that a single *form* of narration – a single, great *compromise-formation*, which brings to light linguistically the conflict between defensiveness and desire – dominates the filmic 'code'. In the last scene of the film, where Michael O'Hara leaves the Crazy House, a wide dolly shot reveals the words 'Fun Fun' painted on it in large block letters. At the last moment oscillation is still operative in the text. The image (Fun Fun) contradicts the sound-track (the moral spoken by the protagonist-narrator). This is the same oscillation between the story that is told and the film that tells it, between a story whose final moral is a mere convention for the benefit of the censors and right-thinking citizens, a counterfeit on the author's part so that the subversive contents could get through safely. A film consciously placed between artifice and illusion – *Fun* with a capital F, *F for Fake*. [13]

NOTES

1   In his book *The Unconscious as Infinite Sets* (1975) Ignacio Matte Blanco reformulates Freud's ideas of the conscious and unconscious as asymmetrical and symmetrical states. The characteristics of the unconscious system described by Freud, that is to say condensation, displacement, replacement of external reality with the psychic one, absence of time and space, absence of contradictions, 'reveal' as Matte Blanco writes, 'the operation of a logic peculiar to this system, whose fundamental distinguishing mark is to treat as symmetrical, relations which in scientific logic are not so considered.' The principle of symmetry (when the converse of any relation is identical with the relation, then the relation is defined as symmetrical) produces a description, in a logical key, of the laws characterizing the unconscious. It is due to Matte Blanco's book that I have been able to see in Welles's picture things I would never otherwise have seen. I also acknowledge the importance to my analysis of Francesco Orlando's literary criticism, particularly his book *Illuminismo e retorica freudiana* (1982), which makes direct reference to Matte Blanco's work.

2   'When the principles of generalisation and symmetry are applied there is no room for the principle of contradiction. . . . Nothing is negated because that which is negated is included in a vaster whole,

and (owing to the principle of symmetry) is identical to that which is affirmed' (Matte Blanco 1975: 46).

3 'When the principle of symmetry is applied the (proper) part is necessarily identical to the whole' (Matte Blanco 1975: 39).

4 In Groupe μ's *Rhétorique générale* (Paris 1970) there is a reference to Bannister's function seen, from linguistic and rhetorical points of view, as 'figures of narration':

> Bannister's role is even more complex in the courtroom scene in *The Lady from Shanghai* by Orson Welles. He is actually the rival of Michael, who is his wife's lover; he becomes Michael's lawyer – joining the functions of both opponent and saviour, but Bannister himself is summoned as a witness and, therefore, he adds to his previous functions that of arbiter. In relation to the actantial pattern we can certainly register a suppression of characters; however, the pluriacting characters who emerge are contradictory and paradoxical.

5 'When the principle of symmetry is applied there cannot be succession' (Matte Blanco 1975: 39).

6 In the third and last version of the script, entitled 'Black Irish' (dated 13 August 1946) Michael tells Elsa that he has been to Africa too. What is curious in this version is that there is no cruise and everything takes place in Long Island between the beach, the villa, the garden, and Bannister's office. In the movie, in the garage sequence, when Elsa invites Michael to take the cruise on her yacht, as a sailor, in the script she actually says: 'You've been to Africa, I'll bet you've never seen Long Island. It will be a new experience.' And Michael becomes the Bannisters' chauffeur.

7 For a more thorough understanding of this analysis, see Chapter III of Matte Blanco (1975), especially pp.54–8.

8 'When the principle of symmetry is applied there can be no relations of contiguity between the parts of a whole' (Matte Blanco 1975: 46).

9 One could think of the 'purse' in Freud (1973: VII) which Dora holds nervously in her fingers and which Freud interprets as a representation of the female genital organ.

10 'When the principle of symmetry is applied, all members of a set or of a class are treated as identical to one another and to the whole set or class' (Matte Blanco 1975: 39).

11 'Once,' Michael says on the night of the picnic, 'off the hump of Brazil I saw the ocean so darkened with blood it was black. . . . A few of us had lines out . . . it was me that had the first strike. A shark it was, and then there was another, another shark again till all about the sea was made of sharks and more sharks still and the water and all. . . . My shark had torn himself from the hook and the

scent or maybe the stain it was, and him bleeding his life away drove the rest of them mad. Then the beasts took to eating each other. In their frenzy they ate at themselves. . . . You could feel the death reeking up off the sea. I never saw anything worse until this little picnic tonight. And, you know, there wasn't one of them sharks in the whole crazy pack that survived.'

12   I refer to Mark Graham's article 'The inaccessibility of *The Lady from Shanghai*' (1981).

13   *F for Fake* (1975) was Orson Welles's last film.

11 Language and the female subject

PATRIZIA VIOLI

EDITORS' INTRODUCTION

The following text is an excerpt from Patrizia Violi's work on
sexual difference in language, a subject on which she recently
published a book, *L'infinito singolare* (1986). Her starting-point is
the conviction that sexual difference is a fundamental dimension
of experience and she speculates on how it presents itself in language and linguistics.

The work was initiated because of a twofold uneasiness: the
'knowledge' of sexual difference arising from experience did not
correspond to full acknowledgement in the linguistic field. Patrizia Violi, who teaches at the University of Bologna and is actively
engaged in semiotics, undertook this work to overcome this
uneasiness and annul a dichotomy. Her endeavour was to merge
two separate areas, 'scientific' and theoretical work in the public
sphere and subjective experience in the personal sphere. She
aimed at analysing their interaction within the semiotic and linguistic systems, to question how sexual difference is symbolized
in language and how linguistic theory takes account of this.
Looked at from another angle, this also means investigating how
female subjectivity can be expressed in language and the symbolic systems, cinema included, which represent it. Using semiotic tools, Patrizia Violi shows the inadequacy of linguistic theories
in accounting for the sexual mark of subjectivity. At a theoretical

level, her research challenges the fact that a large portion of the various theories of language have constructed a notion of the 'subject' in abstract, universal, and transcendental terms, terms which are oblivious of sexual difference. In this sense, Patrizia Violi's work shares a central concern of Anglo-American feminist film theory: the question of the subject and its theorization.

To juxtapose 'language' and the 'female subject' immediately raises certain problems that have to do with the actual use of the terms. Are not the terms 'female subject' (a sexed subject) and 'language' (a formal and symbolic system) incongruous? Indeed, what words can be used to discuss such a subject? If it represents what is repressed in discourse, how can language be used to express precisely what is excluded from language? Here we are caught in the contradiction of feminist theory itself, at once excluded from discourse and imprisoned within it. To find a way out of this paradox, the question of how the subject has been posed within linguistic and semiotic investigations needs to be reconsidered in order to identify the kind of subject these theories describe, and what theoretical limitations they impose on any attempt to sketch the outlines of a different, sexually differentiated, subject.

Not all linguistic and semiotic theories raise the question of the subject and of subjectivity. In theories such as Chomskian generative grammar the focus is always on the abstract level of linguistic competence, and the question of the speaking subject does not even arise. However, at least two major frameworks include a theory of the subject in relation to language and meaning, namely post-Saussurian structural linguistics and semiotic theory of the production of meaning. I will briefly consider these two approaches particularly, to elucidate their implicit theoretical assumptions. Post-Saussurian structural linguistics, especially the work of Emile Benveniste, presents a linguistic model with a strong theory of the subject. Furthermore, the structuralist framework lies behind Lacanian theory: Lacan's subject is derived from the structural linguistic subject. From the outset, Benveniste raises the issue of the subject in language: there is no subject, and no subjectivity, outside language.

It is in language and through language that man is constituted as a subject, because language alone founds itself in reality, in its reality, which is the reality of being, the concept of *ego*. The subjectivity that we are talking about now is the capacity of the speaker to constitute himself as a subject. It is not defined by the consciousness that everybody has of himself, but as the psychic unit which is beyond the totality of our experiences, and which enables consciousness to persist. We view subjectivity, whether we consider it from the psychological or from a phenomenological angle, as nothing but the coming into being of a fundamental property of language. It is *ego* which says *ego*. This is the foundation of subjectivity, which is determined through the linguistic status of person.

(Benveniste 1966; my translation)

Thus, the subject does not exist outside language; it is founded on the act of uttering 'I':

We cannot see man separated from language, and we never see him in the act of inventing it. We cannot see man in himself. In the world we always find a speaking man, a man speaking to another man, and language established the very definition of man. (Benveniste 1966; my translation)

The reality in which the subject is constituted is linguistic reality, the reality of discourse: 'It is in the situation of discourse, where "I" refers to the speaker, that the speaker is constituted as a subject. Therefore it is literally true that the foundation of subjectivity is in the use of language' (Benveniste 1966; my translation).

This emphasis on the constitutive link between language and subjectivity is the crux of Benveniste's theory. Subjectivity can be constituted only within language and its symbolic structure; the subject does not have any 'essence' in itself outside its manifestation in language.

But what kind of subject does Benveniste locate in the symbolic structure of language? It is clear that this subject is nothing more than the *transcendental ego*, an empty space, an abstract principle; it can only be grasped through the traces it leaves in discourse, namely the linguistic category of 'person'. Such a subject cannot, of course, express sexual difference, cannot be a sexually differentiated subject.

In any structuralist theory of the subject, whether Benveniste's or Lacan's, the question of sexual difference is always excised and the subject defined as a universal category, an abstract and asexual principle. However, the transcendental *ego* has a strong tendency to manifest itself as a male subject. If we take Benveniste at his word, as we should, we can clearly see, behind the abstract and transcendental subject, the shape of a man, a male subject. According to Benveniste, the subject *is* its linguistic substance. Now let us quote him again, looking more closely at his linguistic choices: 'In the world we always find a speaking *man*, a *man* speaking to another *man*, and language established the very definition of *man*' (Benveniste 1966; my translation, my italics). This is not a new discovery. In the history of man's philosophy and theory, behind every transcendental ego a male subject is hidden. We, who are not male subjects, are left with no room in which to pose the question of difference: in theory the subject is transcendental and asexual, in language it can only be designated through male categories.

A different version of the transcendental subject which is worth analysing carefully is present in the semiotic model, as set out in Eco's theory of meaning and production of meaning. At first glance, this semiotic framework seems to deal more with the organization of meaning than with the question of the subject. But the notion of code, that is, an active, socially based system regulating human meaning, conceals an implicit theory of the subject, which takes the shape of an essentially semiotic subject. More precisely, I would call such a subject a cultural *subject*, in that it is completely defined by cultural processes, by codes, and by the social production of meaning.

What is interesting and appealing in this perspective is the explicit link between social praxis on the one hand and semiotic processes on the other. Codes and meanings are not abstract immutable entities, but systems undergoing continual change and development, which can only be adequately described through the notion of the social production of meaning. Signs are the result of social activity, therefore they are social forces. Moreover, signs are subject to the process of unlimited semiosis, transforming themselves continuously under the pressure of social change. In this way semiosis is not only the result of social production, it is itself a component of social reality, as real and active as other social forces. But how is the subject defined within this framework? It is defined by the process of semiosis, its boundaries being those of culture itself. Stressing the notion of code, as the conventional and social system regulating the organization of meaning in a given society, Eco approaches the subject through semiotic categories only, explicitly excluding unconscious processes. 'Either the subjects can be defined in terms of semiotic structures or – from this point of view – they do not exist at all' (Eco 1976).

In this version of the transcendental ego, the subject is reduced to the single dimension of social praxis and culture, and it is deprived of its psychic structure, desires, drives, emotions. It could therefore never be a sexually differentiated subject. As Teresa de Lauretis (1982) has pointed out, this is a pre-Freudian perspective 'that reproposes a dichotomous idea of body and mind, matter and intellect, physis and reason'. But there is another important point to be made. The subject's subordination to culture parallels another similar subordination: that of meaning to social codes. In this framework, meaning is only that which is produced by a social process of signification, what can be encoded in a conventionalized system or rules (namely the code) and is *socially* recognized as such. It is impossible even to imagine any further level of meaning, more directly linked to the system of drives, emotions, psychic structure. The level of meaning I am referring to is close to what Julia Kristeva has called 'the semiotic' (*le sémiotique*), indicating a level of pre-symbolic processes. What is problematic and not wholly convincing about Kristeva's notion of 'the semiotic' is its restricted domain of application. The ability to express a level of meaning not yet organized into social codes but still close to drives, desire, and the unconscious, seems to be limited to a poetic vanguard, to 'high cultural' transgression of linguistic codes. 'The semiotic' is only therefore the expression of another cultural form of codification; even if it assumes the form of transgression, transgression is only possible because the code still stands. It seems to me that the level of meaning we are referring to, subject to a pre-symbolic level of organization, is much more pervasive in women's life experience, and, as I will try to show, connected to the experience of sexual difference.

I have argued that the semiotic framework, based on the notion of code and the social production of meaning, may offer a very dynamic concept of signs and meaning as social forces, but restricts the subject to the narrow dimension of culture, excluding the level of unconscious processes. At the same time, and for the very same reason, meaning is likewise reduced to its codified aspect.

To conclude, both structuralist and semiotic frameworks posit the subject as a transcendental category, stripped of both the unconscious and sexual difference. The female subject cannot be situated within these models as existing theories of the subject are unable to grasp the significance of difference. We now face a difficult question, *the* question that arises in all feminist theory, that is how we can define the very object of this theory: the female subject.

We know that the female seems to be precisely that which is removed from language, that which is repressed in discourse, therefore that which is 'unspeakable'. Indeed, if we try to define it, we can only arrive at a negative formulation: 'a woman is something that cannot be'. This is not surprising. If the subject we assume as theoretical paradigm is the transcendental subject, as is the case in our philosophical and psychoanalytic tradition, women cannot but be defined negatively. Within the paradigm of the transcendental ego, it is impossible to frame the question of a different, a female, subject, since that model compels us to excise the idea of difference, which is the basis, the foundation, of the female subject.

On the other hand, it should be clear that the transcendental ego is a 'strong' theoretical category precisely because it is abstract and general; in so far as it is abstract and asexual, it can be postulated as universal. Clearly enough, once such a universal subject has been posited, it becomes impossible to raise the issue of the female subject, because there is no way to articulate the notion of difference, especially sexual difference. We are caught in another paradoxical situation: what makes the subject a universal category is precisely what prevents women from becoming subjects.

Such an impasse is reflected in most feminist theories. Especially in certain elaborations of French feminism, the female subject is only defined by means of a negative: it is the empty space of non-being, which does not, and never could have, a voice. The female subject cannot therefore be approached on the basis of its own specificity, but only as the underside, the sexual counterpart, of the male subject. In this way, the idea of the subject as transcendental ego is implicitly accepted.

The point, of course, is not to define some idealistic 'essence' of what a female subject is, but to find theoretical categories which allow us to frame the questions that are important to us: the question of sexual difference and that of the specificity of our experience, our desire, our grief. We need to pose the question of the subject within a different theoretical framework, since within the transcendental model we have analysed, that which is opposed to being can only be an empty space. As I thought about this problem, a question occurred to me: why has our culture always posited the subject as transcendental ego? In order to answer this question, we have to reconsider the opposition between the categories of the general and the individual.

In the western philosophical tradition, there is a pervasive prejudice against, and a deep fear of, any consideration of the individual as a category of our experience and knowledge. What is 'individual', 'singular', is always relegated to the level of idiosyncrasy, and thus, by definition, outside knowledge and theory. Idiosyncrasy is naturally opposed to and irreducible to theory which aims to reduce the multiplicity and variety of data to a more restricted set of concepts. Once the individual has been reduced to the idiosyncratic, and the idiosyncratic experiences banished outside theory, the subject must then be based only on the category of 'general', and therefore it is posed as the universal and abstract subject. In this way the transcendental ego is created, as an abstract principle, cut off from experience.

I believe that in order to find a model that enables the question of the female subject to be posed, we need to reframe the category of the individual, because the female subject is situated at the intersection between the general and the individual.

It should be clear that by 'individual' I do not mean the idiosyncratic aspect of our experiences, what is specific and peculiar to each human being, but rather the common *form* of our experiences, the *process* which structures our experiences, and which, as form, as process, can be described. The category of the individual is precisely what is *common* to women's idiosyncratic experiences, and is therefore that which makes these experiences communicable and comparable. Indeed, the common form of women's experience can be analysed; it is the specific object of investigation in what Italian feminists have called *autocoscienza*, consciousness of self. The practice of consciousness-raising recognized a similarity, discovered a common process structuring different life experiences. Behind women's varied and idiosyncratic life stories, a basic common form was shown, a general structure which was precisely the *experience of sexual difference*. Sexual difference is a basic category of our experience, and therefore of the very definition of subjectivity and the female subject. One 'becomes a woman' through the experience of sexual difference, which is one of the most personal and secret, and at the same time, one of the most socially and culturally determined experiences.

For this reason, to talk of female subjectivity means to consider simultaneously two different domains, two levels of organization: the social and the psychic. This is because the experience of sexual difference is both encoded in the cultural and semiotic system of representation and meaning, and also inscribed in the structure of unconscious drives. In a framework able to account for the category of the individual, as a way of structuring our experiences and subjectivity, it becomes possible to articulate the question of sexual difference, and therefore that of the female subject.

In all attempts to approach this problem, the ghost of an old dualism seems to appear, a dualism between being and not-being, logos and matter, body and matter. Sexual difference, initially expunged from theory, is then reintroduced in the form of an impossible dualism, which cannot be overcome. But difference is not dualism. If it is true that sexual difference implies an internal duality, we have to emphasize that the reduction of difference to dualism is the result of patriarchal organization, and not the unavoidable consequence of human nature. It is the patriarchal order which cuts off the inner ambivalence of difference and reduces women to only one of the opposite terms, preventing them from being subjects. In this way, women are forced into a dualistic structure, and are obliged to assume the position of the 'negative' pole, the body, the matter.

No easy solution can be found. No myth of an androgynous pacified subject can be evoked. The sign of a contradiction, of dualism, seems to characterize the very nature of female subjectivity. Either described as the double positionality of women's desire, or as the experience of 'the two boundaries of language', the female subject is at the same time a form of being and of not-being. It cannot be contained in only one term, in a single position, unless we fall again into the dualistic opposition imposed on us by tradition, and very often assumed by women themselves, in the impossible search for an uncorrupted nature for the female body.

If we analyse our experience, we may discover our subjectivity to be grounded on the coexistence of a double register of functioning, a double level of meaning, because women are not outside the patriarchal structure, but at the same time do not completely belong to its logic, order, discourse; they are always both within history and elsewhere.

If we look at the problem of language from this perspective, we can make some conclusive remarks. Most feminist attempts to displace the paradoxical situation of female subjectivity in relation to language seem to be caught in the trap set by the paradox of dualism. Some of them explicitly assume the transcendental model, considering 'the subject', like 'man', to be a generic term which can be applied to the male and the female subjects indiscriminately, erasing sexual difference from subjectivity. Consequently, they look for an impossible 'androgynous' language, where all traces of sexual difference are cancelled out. Others set the notion of a different subject on the side of pure negativity, silence, natural sexuality, outside, and not compromised by, patriarchal culture.

As I have tried to show, such a notion cannot define a different subject, constituted as female on the basis of a specific kind of experience, but simply reverts to the negative and sexual counterpart of the male (and universal) subject. The model of the transcendental ego is thus implicitly accepted, and woman becomes its negative limit. In that perspective, woman's language can only take the forms of silence, hysteria, and madness, all symptoms of her failure in terms of male discourse, which condemns her to marginality and to the absence of speech. An impossible choice, obviously, between an emancipation where every difference is erased, and the role of silent spectator in a story which is not her own: either to identify with the power of the phallus and so renounce her different form of subjectivity, or to regress to the further side of the symbolic order, before the mirror phase, before language.

Women must refuse to make this choice, must avoid both being situated within the framework of the transcendental subject, limiting the domain of an individual, differentiated subject, in which difference and contradictions are not played down, but on the contrary, are exhibited. We must also remember that the problem of language cannot be posed only at the linguistic level, in terms of a 'different' language, but that it needs to be reframed at the theoretical level, where the category of female subject can be approached.

PART III
Film production

12 An affectionate and irreverent account of eighty years of women's cinema in Italy

ANNABELLA MISCUGLIO

Translated by Giovanna Ascelle and Rosamund Howe

EDITORS' INTRODUCTION

As well as giving examples of Italian women's critical and theoretical work, we thought it would be useful to give details of their film production as this is unfortunately little known in Britain and the United States. We hope to stimulate interest in this area of cinema and to provide basic documentation for possible exchanges or future studies. We have compiled a filmography to introduce Italian women film-makers and their productions. We also asked Annabella Miscuglio, a protagonist in the field, to write an inside story on women's cinema in Italy, recreating the atmosphere in which it was produced and placing the names from the filmography in context. As a film-maker, Annabella Miscuglio has committed herself to working in the documentary genre, often in collectives. Particularly worthy of mention are: the famous *Processo per stupro* ('Trial for rape') (1978); the controversial documentary *A.A.A. Offresi* (1979), which was censored and the makers prosecuted (the film shows a prostitute with her clients, filmed with her agreement in a candid camera style); and *I fantasmi del fallo* (1980), which documents the making of a pornographic film.

We asked a film-maker rather than a historian to write about women's cinema primarily because we wanted to offer the self-reflexive viewpoint of a woman engaged in making films, and were committed to letting both sides of the camera speak but also for another reason. The situation of Italian feminism, which we have often tried to describe and interpret, with its lack of centralization and its theorizing of practice in a continuous 'deconstructive' process of self-definition, cannot be fitted neatly into any system or systematization and its end-products are therefore hard to categorize. Thus 'paradoxically', for example, women historians of the cinema had not produced a filmography of women's cinema in Italy nor had they done any proper formal studies on it. They had published more on subjects outside their own sphere, such as the films of Chantal Akerman or Marguerite Duras. Rather than through formal studies, the discourse on, and of, Italian women's cinema found expression in the context of film festivals and retrospectives which women were organizing. These events acted as catalysts of discussions and analyses, and were moments of growth and circulation of critical ideas as well as filmic practices (this is often the case in Italy, where discourse on the cinema tends to burst into life, formalize, and circulate in the context of the great number of film festivals which join the presentation of filmic practices with critical discourse). Towards this aim, Annabella Miscuglio was one of the women who committed herself to the circulation of women's cinema and its discourse.

In confronting the problem of documenting women's cinema in Italy, we found 'zones of repression' and 'suppressed knowledges'. The most interesting and glaring lacuna was the lack of analytic studies and information on Elvira Notari and the loss of her films and writings. Elvira Notari (1875–1946) was Italy's first woman director. She was an enterprising and unusually prolific personality who wrote and directed about sixty feature films and a great many shorts in the years from 1906 to 1930. With the filmographic research, some photographic materials and Annabella Miscuglio's text, we want to launch a rediscovery of Elvira Notari's film production and writing and to initiate a reassessment of her role in the history of Italian cinema and the spectrum of women's production.

NAPLES, 1906

In a small, ill-lit workshop Nicola Notari ran his meticulous paintbrush over yards and yards of film. Little bottles of aniline stood on his workbench. Patiently, he had achieved, as a craftsman, the miracle which technology did not bring about until many years later. colour film, Shot after shot, scene after scene, he painted the film, a narrative short, conceived and directed by Elvira Coda Notari.

In only twenty-five years, Elvira Notari energetically scripted and directed fifty-seven features and as many shorts, and started the company Dora Film with her husband Nicola. (Around 1910 they acquired a building with sets and a workshop for developing and printing.) But in 1930 she had to give up her work due to Fascist censorship. This does not mean that Elvira Notari's cinema was politically committed, even though her filmography includes several patriotic titles shot during the First World War: *L'eroismo di un aviatore a Tripoli* (1912), *Figlio del reggimento* (1915), *Sempre avanti, Savoia* (1915), *Gloria ai caduti* (1915). The 'extremely industrious Signora Elvira', described in contemporary news items as a 'very simple woman . . . with a motherly look . . . and a hidden reserve of the moral strength characteristic of southerners' (Paliotti and Grano 1969) made tear-jerkers, films full of dramatic reversals, studded with crimes of passion, betrayal, and torment. So realistic were her films that during a showing of one of them at the Vittoria Cinema in Naples, a man in the audience fired several pistol shots at the screen to kill the 'bad guy'. It was that very realism, that deeply felt depiction of poverty, that annoyed the Fascist regime with its commitment to disseminate an image of Italy as ordered and honest, particularly as Dora Film products were sent across the Atlantic to make millions of Italian emigrants in the USA cry and laugh.

Signora Elvira's films are filled with temptresses, seductresses, and expert vamps, and with weak men ready to risk damnation by committing the most horrendous crimes for their sakes. Her stories were built on the eternal dualism of woman's image: in her dramas there is always a mother, betrayed, abandoned, and desperate, who plays an essential part in re-establishing '*A legge* 'The law'.[1] Woman as occasion of sin and woman as creator of organized society coexist in Notari's imaginary world as a polarization of forces which seem to tear the feminine essence to pieces. I like to think that Elvira was herself living out the conflict between a desire for freedom and her family role. For Elvira believed in the family, to such an extent that she dragged it into her whole cinematic *oeuvre*: even on the set little Eduardo was the 'favourite son' with the pseudonym Gennariello, her husband Nicola took charge of the photography and the sets, and did the developing, printing, and editing with Elvira, who if nothing else, had the chance to liberate her imagination. But the imagination of a Neapolitan keeps one eye on the box-office takings and Elvira, who was also responsible for production, knew her audience well and knew what would draw them into the cinema, the first in Naples to show continuous performances from 9 in the morning till late at night. Most of her films took their titles from popular songs of the day and 'freely draw their inspiration' from them: *Fenesta che lucive* (two versions, 1914 and 1926), *A Marechiaro ce sta na fenesta* (one version in 1913, another in 1924), *Addio mia bella addio, l'armata se ne va* (1915), *Pupatella* (1923), *Reginella* (1923). This was before Italy's big industrial dream-making machine swept away the early regional production companies (of which Dora Film is a typical example) and made Rome the capital of film; and long before computers were used to choose which elements would make a film a success. But even in that completely artisanal phase, next to the question of creating a language for the new medium of expression, a problem arose, which stayed to haunt producers and worry directors: the market.

ROME, 1963

The political and social climate had changed completely and a female *scugnizzo* (Neapolitan urchin) was directing her first film. She was 31, the same age as Elvira Notari at the beginning of her career, and just as determined, just as relentless. But hers was not a sudden appearance on the Italian cultural scene. Unlike Signora Elvira who was self-taught, she had a rich experience behind her, as befits one who aspires to Art. Her training included drama school, cabaret, and radio; she had been an assistant director, co-author of musical comedies, and Fellini's assistant. The 'urchin' was Lina Wertmuller. Her films are too well known to be discussed here.

Ten years later the feminist movement took blind objection to her: her caustic wit, her irreverent angle on national customs which made her caricature aspects of comedy Italian style, the female characters in particular – her work was regarded as an irritation and provocation by the 'woman is beautiful' school which once again separated women from history, to reconsecrate them into myth.

Woman is beautiful. Woman is creativity. Woman takes the camera . . . .

This was a time of great creativity, which brought a huge increase in the number of women involved in film-making. It has left us with the category *women's cinema*, rich in ambiguity and dangers of self-segregation. What is its specific character, I still wonder. Is its difference due to its language and/or content? Its narrative structure? Its production modes? Its point of view?

The concept of a women's cinema first emerged during a period of protest, when women made a link between struggle against cultural misogyny and the appropriation of the means for the transmission of culture and ideology. In tracing its course in Italy, therefore, I feel I should start with the fruitful but strange encounter between cinema and the Women's Movement. In Italy, as in other countries, the appropriation of a means of expression as fundamental to mass culture as cinema grew out of a critique of images of women and of the sexist ideology producing them. It then developed through a variety of concerns, research projects, and experiments, reflecting the richness of the theoretical formulations of the movement itself.

ROME, 1972

At the first big open-air demonstration organized by the Women's Movement, the head of police, with a wave of the Italian flag, gave orders to charge. Truncheons were brought down impatiently on the heads of women who had only been given a few minutes to 'move on to the pavement' and empty the square. As everybody fled, reporters noted with amusement the entire 'women's film collective' taking to their heels, with their cameras on their shoulders. The collective was made up of Rony and Annabella. Ten years later the infernal machine of censorship forced the same two-woman collective to make a much more shameful retreat for having filmed a 'streetwalker' at work. [2]

Documentaries and investigative films, perhaps partly because of their wider accessibility, were the favourite genres of women's cinema at its outset. The subject under investigation was, of course, the condition of women. In line with the conclusions reached during those first years of consciousness-raising, this condition could only be perceived as one of oppression and exploitation, with a hint of 'victimism' here and there. Out of this analysis, a 'militant' cinema developed, which often tended to fall into a kind of 'feminist realism' due to a rather over-schematic and insufficiently dialectical representation of reality. Essentially, this means that in these films ideological discourse overshadows the text instead of being implied in the structure, the new contents fail to find a corresponding mode of expression, the poetry of the images is often blunted by a voice-over commentary which does too much explaining. This problem was the legacy of two tendencies in contemporary Italian production: the Militant Cinema that grew out of the 1968 movement and, to some extent, state cinema.[3] Another point of reference was – and still is – television documentary. This style, modelled on television news, had already polluted the traditional documentary which found its peak in Flaherty and Ivens, and had almost replaced it altogether.

The first documentary work produced by the Centro Sperimentale di Cinematografia was Rony Daopoulo's graduation film, *L'aggettivo donna* (1971). The following films were independent productions: *La lotta non è finita* by the Feminist Film Collective (1972–3), and *Aborto: parlano le donne* (1976) and *Le ragazze di Capoverde* (1976), both by Dacia Maraini.

On another front, unfortunately, feminist cinema liberated the imaginary in such a way as to rediscover the body and 'womanhood' through the same iconography traditionally used to signify it, such as nature, emotion, and magic.

NAPLES, 1974

A group of women warriors wearing transparent, pastel-coloured garments led by a present-day Nemesis – Lina Mangiacapre – shot *Cenerella, psicofavola femminista*. The charismatic leader of the Nemesiache distrusted technical expertise, favouring instead the alchemy of the psycho-photographic process. But in spite of her image as a visionary, Lina Mangiacapre has been the director of the women's section of the Incontri Internazionali del Cinema in Sorrento since 1976.

The medium which made it possible to effect a magical transformation of 'visceral energy' into images was Super-8. *Il mare ci ha chiamate* (1978), *Le Sibille* (1979) and *Follia come Poesia* (1980) are the products of a naïve attempt to find the vanished traces of feminine body-history through the Greek myths which have survived in Neapolitan oral culture.

An interesting aspect of this phase is the use of Super-8 as a more direct and immediate cinematic 'writing', for example in the films made by certain women who moved on to the small format from 35mm and 16mm films. In 1969 Dacia Maraini, who describes herself as a 'writer who occasionally makes films', shot *L'amore coniugale*, a 35mm film which was distributed on the commercial circuit. After she had embraced feminist militancy and made the 16mm documentaries mentioned above, she discovered Super-8 and

> the pleasure of dwelling on that which is unrelated to me but still has the power to give me joy and arouse my curiosity. . . .
> To approach faces, discover them, unveil them, preserve them, touch them: this experience has been full of sensuality and emotional tension. (Maraini 1979)

Mio padre, amore mio (1978) is a journey back into the author's childhood, full of symbolic emphases, whose slow rhythm brings out her narcissistic love of beautiful scenic compositions shot from different angles.

Woman sea. Woman milk. Woman gives herself pleasure. . . .

Narcissism, intimacy, and voyeuristic pleasure characterize some aspects of this cinema which dwells on women's bodies, skin, and eyes transfigured by light, by an erotic look, by a feeling of self-recognition. Sapphic myths find moments of sweet emotion which sometimes achieve a poetic quality. Still, humour and irony are not entirely absent, as in *Affettuosamente ciak* (1979), made by the Alice Guy Collective. This comedy plays on the relationship (unresolved, perhaps particularly for the film-makers) between woman and technology and culture.

But if Super-8 offers the most accessible and cheapest means of representing one's own fantasies and expressing one's own creativity, it also proved to be a way of avoiding the cinema and television production machines which, besides imposing certain production rhythms and modes, blocks the expressive potential of cinema and favours standard products. The small format was also used for research and experimentation, the field in which, to my mind, it gave its best results. A section of Italian independent cinema[4] had adopted it by the end of the 1960s, following the example of Stan Brakhage. The only women who took part in this experiment were Pia Epremian, Patrizia Vicinelli, and Anna Oberto, already committed members of the visual and literary avant-garde. For the 1970s I need only mention *Urbana* by Valentina Berardinone and *Cecily Eating* by Romany Eveleigh, two shorts which show remarkable stylistic rigour.

The idea of a journey back in time, in film format, reminded me of a phenomenon initiated by Nanni Moretti, a young film-maker who had become well known and admired for his work with Super-8, and who then progressed to the big screen. His example influenced all those who had come up against the inevitably exclusive nature of the film industry. Rather than 'doing the rounds' of the production companies, their scripts under their arms, looking for a kind of producer who had become extinct in this period of serious crisis in the film industry, the kind who would invest in a first work, the new film-makers turned to the small format, in spite of all its technological limitations, to make a film, or films, to demonstrate their expressive potential. One example is Gabriella Rosaleva, now highly regarded by the critics, who began her career with *Una Maria del '23* (1979).

1975, RAI-TV

The state television company RAI, still a monopoly, half-opened its large, lazy, sleepy eyes to look at feminist issues. The Women's Movement, in alliance with the Left in the pro-abortion campaign, was at its height, its tendencies expanding, splitting, and multiplying. Women film-makers could bring pressure on RAI-TV both from the inside and the outside. There were a number of women inside; to mention only a few, Loredana Dordi, who had just won the 'De Sica award' at the Venice Film Festival and had made a series entitled *Le donne e la salute* ('Women and Health'), and Marina Tartara, an executive in Rete 2 (Channel 2), who had launched a programme made by and for women. Investigative documentaries included *Marisa della Magliana* by Maricla Boggio, an impassioned portrait of a proletarian woman; *8 Marzo, giornata di festa et di lotta,* by the Arcobaleno co-operative, a history of Women's Day; *Il rischio di vivere* by Anna Carini and Annabella Miscuglio, a study of motherhood from the points of view of desire, culture, and reality. From this point, Women's Movement cinema to some extent abandoned alternative circuits and met a wider public, in spite of objections, as the question of tho rejection of institutions aroused strong feelings at the time. Confrontation with the production system and with television standards demanded relentless commitment. The bureaucratic slowness of a gigantic organism, the obstruction and sexism of unmotivated technicians worn down by a business routine which treated them as robots – all this made a lot of women decide to work freelance[5] and set up independent co-operatives where they could maintain the illusion of autonomy and the determination to fight. They began to learn the same lessons as their predecessors, such as Wertmuller and Cavani, and all the other women who carried on stubbornly, day after day, building up a professional identity which could only achieve recognition and gain stimulus for growth through the TV set and through contact with the public and the critics.

In 1977 a women's editorial team at RAI managed to launch *Si dice donna,* a weekly television news programme.

> The model, which was not chosen in advance, turned out to be the most conventional possible, similar to many previous RAI investigative programmes. But the content had a quite unprecedented force: the words that now came out of women's long historic silence had never previously been brought into focus, while the faces of real women (unlike the ones on television commercials) had a shattering strength. . . . But a weekly programme has to offer information and its main requirement is news. But from a feminist perspective, what makes news?
>
> (Capomazza 1981)

Thus Tilde Capomazza, editor-in-chief of the programme, expressed her difficulties over finding 'news' in women's daily lives, feelings, and actions. The weekly broadcast, which had been shown in peak viewing time by the RAI management in response to demands and pressure by female viewers, after going up in the ratings, was suddenly suppressed in 1981. It was partly for political reasons that television time was barred to programmes intended to criticize the condition of women. (During that same period we were impotent witnesses of an erosion of democracy and the reversal of many working-class victories; the Women's Movement would not speak out on these issues although women were the first to suffer.) In fact censorship hit a lot of RAI programmes, among them *A.A.A. Offresi*, made by the women's collective which had shot *Un processo per stupro* ('Trial for rape') in 1978. But new trends in state television production were mainly influenced by the expansion of private television companies which opened the way for a battle for ratings. Data on viewing patterns showed that audiences wanted entertainment and escape from their troubles, not to be made aware. This was not new in itself, but competition gave it a new importance. It meant that entertainment triumphed, at least for a few years until, once again, it was recognized that you can entertain people at the same time as giving them information and making them think.

ROME, 1977

Io sono mia.[6] Women's slogans arrive on the big screen. This was the first big feminist venture into commercial cinema. The promoter was the tiny, passionate Lù Leone, who found an all-women crew. It took two or three years' preparation to win over producers and smooth out the problems of collective film-making. But a producer was found. Following the publishing industry, the film industry had guessed that 'women sell' and invested accordingly. The investment paid off in terms of popularity with a public generally sceptical of women's cinema and Italian productions.

Unfortunately, the film did not turn out well, in spite of the good faith and serious intentions of all those who took part in making it under the direction of Sofia Scandurra. It was a defeat for professionalism, built up over the years, by ideology. The story was constructed rhetorically; the characters were empty vehicles for over-explicit messages, symbolic puppets devoid of emotion and without psychological depth, and thus incapable of involving the spectator. Because it was so schematic, the intention behind the film – to denounce and provoke – irritated the spectator.

Liliana Cavani's *Al di là del bene e del male* and Lina Wertmuller's *La fine del mondo nel nostro solito letto in una notte piena di poggia* came out in the same year. Still the only famous women in the national film industry, though not insensitive to feminist issues, they would not let themselves be taken over. Wertmuller, always sensitive to socio-cultural change, in keeping to her own style, portrayed the crisis of the couple, in a dead-end and waiting for a regeneration which never came. The film appeared to be a metaphor for the dead-end Italian politics had entered, ruling and revolutionary sides alike, just before the economic crisis and the 'leaden years'.

In the same year two other women, Elda Tattoli and Giovanna Gagliardo, were wandering anxiously around the world of film production. The former had made *Pianeta Venere* in 1972, which tells the story of a woman doubly oppressed by her class and her sex. It was not liked, especially because, in the end, the Marxist patriarchs are responsible for the protagonist's liberation. Still, in sometimes chilling scenes, the film portrays the cultural, social, and political contradictions which women faced in that period of deep transformation. Tattoli had to wait a full twelve years before she could make her second film, which still has no distributor.

Giovanna Gagliardo has also had to face the problem of distribution. She made *Maternale* in 1978. Through a description of food, actions, and looks, it shows how excessive maternal love can be an impediment to a child's development. The film was produced by RAI-TV, as also was *Improvviso* by Edith Bruck.

RAI-TV's intervention in the production of *auteur* cinema was a rescue operation in a climate of crisis – a crisis of the market (posters advertising a large number of films were put up and taken down within a few days because business managers were not satisfied with the box-office takings) and a crisis in financial investment (producers who had not moved abroad such as Ponti, De Laurentis, and Grimaldi favoured 'off-the-peg' cinema designed solely to produce commodities for immediate consumption and a quick return on capital). Comedy Italian-style declined even further into the most squalid vulgarity, while 'quality cinema' kept the national flag flying thanks to the 'sacred cows' of Great Cinema.

The old-style producer, who financed large-audience films and was also prepared to take on new people, and thus bring up a new generation, had long since disappeared. State television had taken on the role of talent scout. While it could not always guarantee cinema distribution, it could at least provide a showing on TV, although sometimes a few years after a film had been completed. Of course it never took risks although the new directors were all, by and large, experienced. They had worked as film critics or scriptwriters or in television production (current affairs, serials), as assistant directors – they were the 'sons – or wives – of art'.

This development took place at the same time as the explosion of private television companies which quickly became big business, but were not, for all that, free from political interference. This completely changed modes of consumption. For the first time in Italy, spectator time ceased to be the same as film time: terrorized into staying at home by the mass media, a sounding box for political terrorism and day-to-day violence, people watched advertising interrupted by scenes from a film. Why go out at night and risk being mugged or shot at when TV churns out war live and free of cost in time and money? You could watch a show as you ate your spaghetti, or 'take part' in a quiz programme while you got the dinner ready. By this time the welfare economy, though in crisis, had made so many television sets available that we could peacefully enjoy our favourite serial or soap opera one after another while our husbands revelled in the discovery of women's wrestling and our sons, depending on their age, were either absorbed by the elating eroticism of a ball kicked on a green field or by the intergalactic wars fought by electronic figures made in Japan and invading the toy shops.

The television empire, now a competitive system, took the place of the film club, hitherto the only venue for watching films on the commercial fringe and for experiencing the history of cinema. Film clubs had made up for the inadequacies of an official cultural policy which was not sensitive to the 'seventh art' and did not subsidize its development in public institutions (universities, schools, film libraries). With the end of the film club the last stronghold of independent cinema collapsed. With festivals now the only remaining shop windows, and these reserved for an élite audience, the hunt for financiers, public or private, was resumed.

To put a film together, in the sense of finding the money, is an adventure for any director, a test of patience and self-confidence. For a woman film-maker the search for finance is fraught with such horrifying experiences that only a lively sense of humour can save her from being destroyed by it. The younger, war-hardened women have developed this quality. In the 1980s a new, young cinema was born, with a new, young generation free from the ideological and political tension which chackled the previous one, a generation which has joined the production system and is ready to challenge the market and compromise if necessary.

Women's cinema of the 1980s belongs to the category known in Italy as 'young cinema'.

This 'phenomenon' which is still in full flow and is still rather obscure should really be discussed at length. Although people often talk about 'young cinema', the meaning of the term is not completely clear. Young in years? Young in the new forms it looks for? Young in content? What now seems undoubtedly young, with 'young' meaning 'new', is the name. Perhaps we have finally understood that today only those who have a name – and a target – can have access to production. 'The main vehicle of your non-freedom is your name. . . . Those who do not know it have no power over you' (E. Canetti).

NOTES

1   'A legge directed by Elvira Notari; from a story by Pacifico Veneto, script: Elvira Notari; cinematography: Nicola Notari; music: Nicola and Elvira Notari; cast: Gennariello, Giuseppe de Blasio, Lisa Cava; production and studio: Dora Film; country of production: Italy (1920), black and white, silent, 1,300 m (from Miscuglio and Daopoulo 1980).

2   Reference to the video A.A.A. Offresi (1980), by M. Grazia Belmonti, Anna Carini, Rony Daopoulo, Paola De Martiis, Annabella Miscuglio, and Loredana Rotondo. The documentary is an enquiry into male behaviour during encounters with a prostitute. It was banned a few minutes before it went on the air by direct government intervention, after about a hundred protests had been made by private citizens and associations for safeguarding morality in television, none of whom had seen it. The film-makers were brought to trial on charges of 'interfering in private life' and 'aiding prostitution'. Only the protagonist was aware of the camera placed in her flat. Her clients, though unaware of it, were shot in such a way as to be

unidentifiable. At the trial, the film-makers were discharged but the negative of the film was confiscated and it cannot be shown. The outcome of the appeal is pending.

3   Militant Cinema started with the same objectives as the American Newsreel Collective. State cinema is an organism which advances money for the production of films after the scripts have been examined by a committee. The finance provided covers the costs of only extremely low-budget films. Distribution is abysmal. A few films of a clearly political nature, but of little artistic interest, were made in this way in the 1970s.

4   A movement inspired by American underground cinema with which it is in close contact.

5   An RAI production formula which entrusts the production process to a private company or co-operative, while financing the project in full. Generally an RAI officer with a supervisory function oversees the setting up and making of the film. The advantage of this type of contract is that it allows the possibility of free choice of technicians from outside RAI; under other systems they are officially and casually allocated.

6   *Io sono mia* directed by Sofia Scandurra; from the novel *Donne in guerra* by Dacia Maraini; script: Sofia Scandurra, Lù Leone; cinematography: Nurith Aviv; editing: Gabriella Cristiani; music: Giovanna Marini; cast: Stefania Sandrelli, Maria Schneider, Michele Placido, Anna Henkel, Francisco Rabal; production: Clesi Cinematografica; country of production: Italy (1977), colour, 35 mm.

13 Filmography: women in film in Italy

GIULIANA BRUNO AND MARIA NADOTTI

This filmography is by no means definitive. It does not intend to exhaust the diverse panorama of Italian women's film production, but rather intends to provide a starting-point and a stimulus for further research on Italian film-makers.

The editors would like to thank Annabella Miscuglio and Adriana Monti for their valuable collaboration.

FRANCESCA ARCHIBUGI

Riflesso condizionato (1982), colour, 16 mm, 28 min.
La guerra appena finita (1983), colour, 16 mm, 24 min.
Un sogno truffato (1984), colour, 16 mm, 26 min.
La piccola avventura (1985), colour, 16 mm, 20 min.
Il vestito più bello (1985), colour, 16 mm, 17 min.
Mignon é partita (in production), colour, 35 mm.

DONATELLA BAGLIVO

Andrej Tarkovskij in 'Nostalghia' (1984), colour, 16 mm.

ANNA BALDAZZI

Mussolini (1969), colour, 16 mm, 45 min.
Greta Garbo (1974), colour, 16 mm, 30 min.

Il vestito più bello (1985), a film by F. Archibugi

Haiti (1974), colour, 16 mm, 60 min.

Since 1976 she has been working as a producer and director for Italian television and, in this capacity, has made a number of documentaries including: *Le donne casalinghe, La donna e lo sport, Il femminismo, Un problema una pillola, Baci da Cattolica*.

ARMENIA BALDUCCI

Sul decentramento culturale (1970), black and white, 16 mm, 40 min.
La tenda in piazza (1971), black and white, 16 mm, 50 min.
Reggio Calabria (1972), black and white, 16 mm, 115 min.
Destino casalinga (1975), black and white, 16 mm, 50 min.
Donne da slegare (1976), black and white, 16 mm, 40 min.
Amo non amo (1979), colour, 16 mm, 110 min.
Star System (1981), colour, 16 mm, 110 min.

VALENTINA BERARDINONE

Silent Invasion (1971), black and white and tinted, 16 mm, 15 min.
Letture numero tre (1972), colour and black and white, Super-8, 18 min.
Viaggio sentimentale (1972), colour, Super-8, 18 min.
Urbana (1973), black and white, Super-8, 16 min.
Eventi (1974), black and white, Super-8, 10 min.
Imago (1975), black and white, 16 mm, 13 min.
A vista d'occhio (1976), colour, silent, Super-8, 15 min.
Euridice (1979), colour, silent, Super-8, 15 min.
Superficiale (1982), colour, Super-8, 30 min.

ALESSANDRA BOCCHETTI

Della conoscenza (1968), colour, 16 mm, 35 min.

Between 1970 and 1974 she directed about twenty educational, promotional and short films. Between 1978 and 1981 she directed *Si dice donna*, a series of investigative programmes for Italian television including: *Marguerite Duras, Olympia des Gouges, Piera degli Esposti, Giuliana Rocchi Poeta, La madre della sposa, Mamma Natale*.

MARICLA BOGGIO

Productions for Italian television including:
Marisa della Magliana (1976), black and white, 16 mm, 55 min.
Sono arrivati quattro fratelli (1979), colour, 16 mm, 60 min.
Farsi uomo oltre la droga (1981–2), colour, 16 mm, five 60-min instalments.
Natuzza Evolo (1985), colour, 16 mm, 90 min.

MARIA BOSIO

La verità non si dice mai (1984), colour, 16 mm, 90 min.

She has directed over thirty television programmes, including:
Ombre rosa, Sotto il segno di Valentina, L'altro teatro, Film dal vero: il processo di Catanzaro.

EDITH BRUCK

Improvviso (1979), colour, 35 mm, 90 min
Quale Sardegna (1983), colour, 35 mm, 60 min (for Italian television)

She is working on a film of Camon's novel *Un altare per la madre*, colour, 35 mm.

ISABELLA BRUNO

Presenze (1974), colour, Super-8, 3.30 min.
On baille, on sort et c'est la mort (1974), colour, Super-8, 6 min.
L'ossessione del domani (1974), colour, Super-8, 3.37 min.
Fissione nucleica (1974), black and white, 16 mm, 30 min.
Cinque donne di chiacchiere (1974), black and white, 16 mm, 60 min.
L'alternativa numero-I (1975), colour, Super-8, 10 min.
Con la partecipazione di (1975), black and white, Super-8, 3 min.
Finchè il fuoco non diventi che luce (1975), colour, Super-8, 15 min.
Donne, emergete (1975), colour, Super-8, 13 min.
Ma il cielo è sempre più blu (1976), colour, Super-8, 20 min.
È solo a noi che sta la decisione (1976), colour, Super-8, 40 min.
La cavia (1976), colour, Super-8, 15 min.
Chi è dentro è dentro, chi è fuori è fuori (1977), colour, Super-8, 35 min. (co-directed with F. Giulie).

Since 1977 she has made programmes and investigative documentaries for television including: *Tutti in scena* (1980), *Arrivano i vostri ovvero l'avventurosa storia del'western all'italiana* (1983).

MARIELLA BUSCEMI

Videoperformance (1978), black and white, video, multimedia, 60 min (co-directed with Arcangelo Mazzoleni).
L'occhio selvaggio (1981), colour, video, multimedia, 60 min (co-directed with Arcangelo Mazzoleni).

MICHELA CARUSO

Casa, dolce casa (1978), colour, Super-8, 30 min.

STEFANIA CASINI AND FRANCESCA MARCIANO

Lontano da dove (1983), colour, 35 mm, 90 min.

LILIANA CAVANI

Incontro notturno (1961), short film
L'evento (1962), short film.
Storia del terzo Reich (1963), 4-hour compilation film for TV.
L'età di Stalin (1963), compilation film for TV.
La casa in Italia (1964), 4-hour television programme.
Philippe Pétain processo a Vichy (1965), 60-min television programme.
La donna nella resistenza (1965), investigative television documentary.
Gesù mio fratello (1965), investigative television documentary.
Il giorno della pace (1965), investigative television documentary.
Francesco d'Assisi (1966), black and white, 16 mm, 115 min.
Galileo (1968), colour, 35 mm, 110 min.
I cannibali (1969), colour, 35 mm, 88 min.
L'ospite (1971), colour, 16 mm, 90 min.
Milarepa (1973/4), colour, 16 mm, 108 min.
Il portiere di notte (1974), colour, 35 mm, 115 min.
Al di là del bene e del male (1977), colour, 35 mm, 110 min.
La pelle (1980), colour, 35 mm, 110 min.

Oltre la porta (1982), colour, 35 mm, 100 min.
Interno Berlinese (1985), colour, 35 mm, 120 min.

GAIA CERIANA

Le crisalidi (1981), colour, three 45-min episodes for television (co-directed with Chantal Personé).

COLLETTIVO ALICE GUY

Affettuosamente ciak (1979), colour, Super-8, 104 min.

FRANCESCA COMENCINI

Pianoforte (1984), colour, 35 mm, 110 min.

BIANCA CONTI ROSSINI

La salita, short film.
Ave . . . Maria (1984), colour, 16 mm, 5 min.

ESTER DE MIRO

Nella città d'ardesia, la poesia (1979), colour, video, 60 min.

GIORGIA DE' NEGRI AND SERENELLA ISIDORI

Anaïs Nin (1979), black and white, 20 min.

ANNA DI FRANCISCA

Luoghi comuni: bar (1981), colour, 16 mm, 11 min.

LOREDANA DORDI

Fratelli (1985), colour, 35 mm, 100 min.

She has been working for Italian television since 1968 and in this capacity has made a number of documentaries and films on women's lives, including *Riprendiamoci la vita* and *Essere madre a 40 anni*.

PIA EPREMIAN

Proussade (1967), colour, Super-8, 60 min.
Pistoletto & Sotheby (1968), colour, 8 mm, 10 min.
Doppio suicidio (1969), colour, 8 mm, 15 min.
Il vino e la pigrizia (1969), colour, 8 mm, 10 min.
Antonio delle nevi (1970), colour, 8 mm, 20 min.
Medea (1970), black and white and colour, 8 mm, 25 min.
Infiniti sufficienti (1971), black and white, 8 mm, 15 min.

PAOLA FALOJA

I manichini (1965), black and white, 35 mm, 12 min.
Liberty (1966), colour, 35 mm, 15 min.
Miti d'oggi: i giocattoli (1967), colour, 35 mm, 14 min.
Il ragazzo motore (1967), black and white, 35 mm, 12 min.
Il riso (1968), colour, 35 mm, 15 min.
Panopticum (1969), colour, 35 mm, 13 min.

Since 1975 she has been working for television, where she has made documentaries on sociological and scientific subjects, including two episodes of *Si dice donna*.

CHIARA FERRIGNO AND CARMEN ROBUSTELLI

Il regalo (1982), colour, 16 mm, 7 min.

CLAUDIA FLORIO

Occhei, occhei (1984), colour, 35 mm, 105 min.

GIOVANNA GAGLIARDO

Maternale (1978), colour, 35 mm, 110 min.
Il sogno dell'altro (1980), 60 min, made for television.
Via degli specchi (1982), colour, 35 mm, 90 min.

She is also the scriptwriter of films directed by Miklos Jancso.

LILIANA GIANNESCHI

Sotto il muro (1978), black and white, 16 mm, 12 min.

(left to right) Benedetta Pantoli and Carla Gravina in *Maternale* (1978), a film by G. Gagliardo

(left to right) Nicole Garcia and Milva in *Via degli specchi* (1982), a film
by G. Gagliardo

(left to right) Heinz Bennet and Nicole Garcia in *Via degli specchi* (1982),
a film by G. Gagliardo

FIORELLA INFASCELLI

Ladra di sogni (1968), short film.
Ritratto di donna distesa (1980), colour, video, 55 min.
Pa (1983), colour, video, 14 min.
Maschere (in production), colour, 35 mm.

ANNA LAJOLO

Various independent experimental films including the following (all co-directed with Guido Lombardi):

D – Non diversi giorni si pensa splendessero alle prime origini del nascente mondo o che avessero temperatura diversa (1970), black and white, 16 mm, 40 min.

E – Là il cielo e la terra si univano, là le quattro stagioni si ricongiunge-vano, là il vento e la pioggia si incontravano (1972), black and white, 16 mm, 75 min.

I blues – Cronache del sentimento politico (1975), colour and black and white, 16 mm, 70 min.

Documentaries (co-directed with Alfredo Leonardi and Guido Lombardi):

E nua ca simu a forza du mundu (1971), black and white, 16 mm, 65 min.

Il fitto dei padroni non lo paghiamo più (1972), black and white, video ½″, 35 min.

Quartieri popolari di Roma (1973), black and white, video ½″, 50 min.

Carcere in Italia (1973), black and white, video ½″, 50 min.

Lottando la vita, emigrati italiani a Berlino (1975), black and white, video ½″, 105 min.

L'isola dell'isola (1977), black and white, video ½″, 90 min.

Il lavoro contro la vita (Porto Marghera) (1979), colour, video ¾″ U-matic, 107 min.

Videos (with Guido Lombardi):

La Zattera di Babele (1982), colour, video ¾″ U-matic, 60 min.

Nozze immaginarie nella città di Genz (1983), colour, video ¾″ U-matic, 90 min.

Between 1979 and 1985 she and Guido Lombardi co-directed thirty-four programmes for Italian television.

LÙ LEONE

Melinda strega per forza (1976), colour, 35 mm, 13 min.
Il battesimo (1979), colour, 35 mm, 20 min.
La storia di una donna e di un soldato (1981), colour, 16 mm, 13 min.

She has worked as assistant director for De Sica, Lizzani, Risi, Soldati, Pietrangeli, Comencini, and others. She produced Marco Bellocchio's films and *Io sono mia*, directed by Sofia Scandurra.

ANTONELLA LICATA

Ultima festa galante (1982), colour, 16 mm, 10 min.

MUZZI LOFFREDO

Occhio nero, occhio biondo, occhio felino (1984), colour, 35 mm, 90 min.
Un pipistrello sotto il cuore (in production), colour, 35 mm.

LINA MANGIACAPRE AND LE NEMESIACHE

Cenerella, psicofavola femminista (1974), colour, Super-8, 50 min.
Il mare ci ha chiamate (1978), colour, Super-8, 30 min.
Le Sibille (1979), colour, Super-8, 30 min.
Anti-strip (1979), colour, Super-8, 15 min.
Follia come Poesia (1980), colour, Super-8, 60 min.
Riccio capriccio (1981), colour, Super-8 and slides, 40 min.
Eliogabalo (1983), colour, video, 11 min.
Didone non è morta (in production), colour, 35 mm.

CECILIA MANGINI

All'armi siam fascisti (1962), black and white, 35 mm, 125 min.
Essere donne (1964), black and white, 16 mm, 35 min.
Domani vincerò (1966), black and white, 35 mm, 27 min.
Brindisi '66 (1966), black and white, 35 mm, 27 min.
L'altra faccia del pallone (1972), black and white, 16 mm, 48 min.

She has also directed thirty-five short films including:

Ignoti alla città (1958), colour, 35 mm, 15 min.
Firenze di Pratolini (1959), colour, 35 mm, 20 min.
Divino amore (1960), colour, 35 mm, 15 min.
La canta delle marane (1961), colour, 35 mm, 15 min.
Stendali (1962), colour, 35 mm, 15 min.
O Trieste del mio cuore (1964), black and white, 35 mm, 15 min.
Felice Natale (1965), colour, 35 mm, 15 min.
Tommaso (1966), black and white, 35 mm, 15 min.
La scelta (1967), black and white, 35 mm, 20 min.
Spadino (1971), colour, 35 mm, 15 min.
Mi chiamo Claudio Rossi (1972), colour, 35 mm, 15 min.

DACIA MARAINI

L'amore coniugale (1969/70), colour, 35 mm, 100 min.
Aborto: parlano le donne (1976), black and white, 16 mm, 50 min.
Le ragazze di Capoverde (1976), black and white, 16 mm, 50 min.
Ritratti di donne africane (1976), colour, 16 mm, 3 hrs.
Mio padre amore mio (1978), colour, Super-8, 25 min.
La bella addormentata nel bosco (1978), colour, Super-8.
Giochi di latte (1979), colour, Super-8, 25 min.
Elmolo (1980), colour, 16 mm, 120 min.
Lo scialle azzurro (1982), colour, Super-8, 60 min (co-directed with
    Paola Raguzzi and Giustina Laurenzi).

G. FIORELLA MARIANI

Homo Sapiens (1978), black and white, 35 mm, 55 min.
Maria Callas (1980), black and white, 16 mm, 60 min (made for
    Italian television).
Omaggio a Toscanini (1982), black and white and colour, 16 mm,
    180 min (made for Italian television).
Ingrid in Italia (1983), black and white and colour, 35 mm, 20 min.
Noi per loro (1984), colour, 16 mm, 25 min.
Missione Africa (1984), colour, 16 mm, 30 min.
Cronaca di una spedizione di pace (1985), colour, 16 mm, 90 min.

LORENZA MAZZETTI

K (1954), black and white, 16 mm, 40 min.
Together (1955), black and white, 35 mm, 60 min.

Veronique, protagonist of *A.A.A. Offresi* (1979), a film by M.G. Belmonti, A. Carini, R. Daopoulo, P. De Martiis, A. Miscuglio and L. Rotondo

ANNABELLA MISCUGLIO

L'aggettivo donna (1971), black and white, 16 mm, 60 min (co-directed with Rony Daopoulo).

Ritratti, Canti illuminati, Maitreja, Fughe lineari (1975/6), colour and black and white, Super-8, short films with music.

La lotta non è finita (1972), black and white, 16 mm, 30 min (documentary co-directed with Rony Daopoulo).

Il rischio di vivere (1976), black and white, 16 mm, (investigative piece co-directed with Anna Carini).

Ciak, le donne si raccontano (1976) (made for television in collaboration with Rony Daopoulo and Danielle Turone).

Frammenti di una vita d'eroina (1978), black and white, video, 45 min (co-directed with Maria Grazia Belmonti, Anna Carini, Rony Daopoulo, Paola De Martiis).

Processo per stupro (1978), black and white, 16 mm, 60 min (co-directed with M.G. Belmonti, A. Carini, R. Daopoulo, P. De Martiis, L. Rotondo).

A.A.A. Offresi (1979), black and white, video, 60 min (co-directed with D.G. Belmonti, A. Carini, R. Daopoulo, P. De Martiis, L. Rotondo).

(Above) *Processo per stupro* (1978), a film by M.G. Belmonti, A. Carini, R. Daopoulo, P. De Martiis, A. Miscuglio and L. Rotondo

(Below) *Ritratti* (1975/6), a film by A. Miscuglio

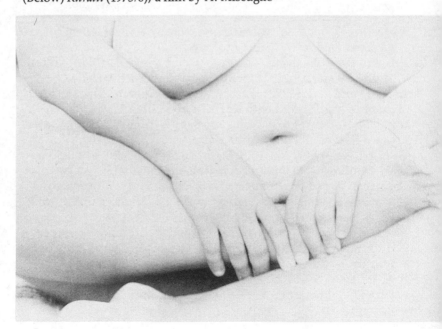

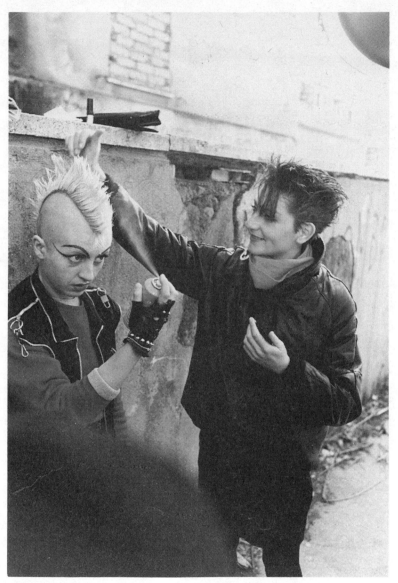

Percorsi metropolitani (1983), a film by A. Miscuglio

Percorsi metropolitani (1983), a film by A. Miscuglio

Morso d'amore, viaggio attraverso il tarantismo pugliese (1980), colour, video, 60 min (co-directed with R. Daopoulo and M.G. Belmonti).

I fantasmi del fallo (1980), colour, video, 60 min (co-directed with R. Daopoulo and M.G. Belmonti).

Maschio si nasce . . . non si diventa (1980), colour, video, 60 min (co-directed with R. Daopoulo and M.G. Belmonti).

Coena cypriani (1981), colour, 16 mm, 90 min.

Graffi sulla città (1982), colour, video, 30 min.

Addio del passato (1982), colour, video, 30 min.

La memoria (1982), colour, video, 30 min.

Percorsi metropolitani (1983), colour, 30 min. (documentary).

Storie di ieri, vita di oggi (1983), colour, video, 60 min.

Passione e lacrime (1984), colour, video, 30 min.

Psicofarmaci sì no (1985), colour, 16 mm, 60 min (investigative television documentary).

Droga da weekend (1985), colour, 16 mm, 60 min (investigative television documentary co-directed with Annalisa Merlina).

ADRIANA MONTI

Trame (1982), colour, video, 20 min.

Una scuola di cinema a Milano (1983), colour, video, 30 min.

Scuola senza fine (1983), black and white, 16 mm, 40 min.

Tracce sulla pelle incantata (1984), video compilation, colour and black and white, 15 min.

Spazi vocali (1984), colour, video, 30 min.

Gentile Signora (in production), colour, 16 mm.

She works for Italian television and has been Comencini's assistant director.

ELVIRA NOTARI

Gli arrivederci (1906), black and white, twenty-two episodes of varying lengths.

L'accalappiacani (1909), black and white, silent, 40 m.

Il processo Cuocolo (1909), black and white, silent, c. 1,000 m.

Maria Rosa di Santa Flavia, (1910), black and white, silent, 280 m.

Fuga del gatto (1910), black and white, silent, 600 m.

Ritorna all'onda (1912), black and white, silent, 1,000 m.

La figlia del Vesuvio (1912), black and white, silent, 700 m.

Publicity still of *Ritorna all'onda* (1912), a film by E. Notari

I nomadi (1912), black and white, silent, 600 m.

Guerra italo-turca tra scugnizzi napoletani (1912), black and white, silent, 500 m.

L'eroismo di un aviatore a Tripoli (1912), black and white, silent, 700 m.

Povera Tisa, povera madre (1913), black and white, silent, 700 m.

Carmela, la sartina di Montesanto (1913), black and white, silent, 1,100 m.

Ciccio ò pizzaiuolo d' o carmine, or Errore giudiziario (1913), black and white, silent, 1,000 m.

Tricolore (1913), black and white, silent, *c.* 1,000 m.

Fenesta che lucive (first version 1914), black and white, silent, 1,000 m.

A Marechiaro ce sta na fenesta (first version 1913/15), black and white, silent, 1,200 m.

Addio mia bella addio, l'armata se ne va (1915), black and white, silent, *c.* 1,200 m.

La fata di Borgo Loreto (1915), black and white, silent, 1,200 m.

Figlio del reggimento (1915), black and white, silent, 1,200 m.

Sempre avanti, Savoia (1915), black and white, silent, 1,200 m.

Nano rosso (1916), black and white, silent, *c.* 1,600 m.

Mandolinata a mare (1916), black and white, silent, 1,500 m.

Gloria ai caduti (1915), black and white, silent, 1,100 m.

Barcaiuolo d'Amalfi (1917), black and white, silent, 1,500 m.

La maschera del vizio (1917), black and white, silent, 1,500 m.

Gnesella (1917), black and white, silent, 1,300 m.

Pusilleco addiruso or Rimpianto (1918), black and white, silent, *c.* 1,300 m.

Chiarina la modista (1918), black and white, silent, *c.* 1,300 m.

Il lampionario di porto (Rosa la pazza) (1918), black and white, silent, 1,300 m.

Medea di Porta Medina (1918), black and white, silent, 1,300 m.

'A piedigrotta (1919), black and white, silent, 1,300 m.

'A legge (1919), black and white, silent, *c.* 1,300 m.

'A mala nova (1920), black and white, silent, *c.* 1,300 m.

Gennariello il poliziotto (1920), black and white, silent, *c.* 1,300 m.

Luciella (1921), black and white, silent, *c.* 1,300 m.

Il figlio del galeotto (1921), black and white, silent, *c.* 1,300 m.

Core 'e frate (1921), black and white, silent, *c.* 1,300 m.

Cielo celeste (1922), black and white, silent, *c.* 1,300 m.

Cielo 'e Napule (1922), black and white, silent, *c.* 1,300 m.

Napoli terra d'amore (1928), a film by E. Notari

'A santa notte (1922), black and white, silent, *c.* 1,300 m.
Scugnizza (1923), black and white, silent, *c.* 1,300 m.
Pupatella (1923), black and white, silent, *c.* 1,300 m.
È piccerella (1922), black and white, silent, 1,304 m.
Sotto o carcere di San Francisco or 'N galera (1922), black and white,
    silent, *c.* 1,500 m.
Il miracolo della Madonna di Pompei (1922), black and white, silent,
    1,289 m.
Reginella (1923), black and white, silent, *c.* 1,300 m.
Cuppè d'a morte (1923), black and white, silent, *c.* 1,400 m.
A Marechiaro ce sta na fenesta (second version 1924), black and
    white, silent, *c.* 1,500 m.
Nfama (voglio a tte) (1924), black and white, silent, *c.* 1,500 m.
Otto e novanta (1924), black and white, silent, *c.* 1,300 m.
Mettite ll'avvocato (1924), black and white, silent, *c.* 1,500 m.
Trionfo cristiano (1925), black and white, silent, *c.* 1,300 m.
Fenesta che lucive (second version 1926), black and white, silent, *c.*
    1,500 m.
La leggenda di Napoli (1928), black and white, silent, *c.* 1,500 m.
Napoli terra d'amore (1928), colour, silent, *c.* 1,500 m.
Napoli sirena delle canzoni (1929), colour, silent, *c.* 1,500 m.
Duie paravise (1929), black and white, silent, 1,500 m.
Passa a bandiera (1930), black and white, silent, *c.* 1,500 m.

VIRGINIA ONORATO

All'Alfa (1969), black and white, 16 mm, 60 min (Militant Cinema
    documentary).
L'ultimo uomo di Sara (1972), colour, 35 mm, 90 min.

Since 1972 she has been working for Italian television where she
has made a number of documentaries and investigative programmes including *Rapporti tra donne israeliane e palestinesi*.

ROSALIA POLIZZI

I mille volti di Eva (1978), 16 mm, 55 min.

She has also made documentaries for Italian television including
Madre ma come (1977) and *Incontro con Camilla Ravera* (1980).

LUDOVICA RIPA DI MEANA

I ragazzi di Santa Domenica (1971), black and white, 16 mm, 45 min.
Palazzeschi (1971), black and white, 16 mm, 20 min.
Carlo Emilio Gadda (1972), colour, 16 mm, 60 min.
Il laboratorio dello storico (1973), black and white, 16 mm, 300 min.
La donna che lavora (1973), black and white, 16 mm, 30 min.
Quando il bambino si ammala (1974/5), black and white, 16 mm, 240 min.
Gruppo di parole (1975), black and white, 16 mm, 30 min.
Odin Teatret (1976), colour, 16 mm, 60 min.
Ritratto di Silvana Pampanini (1977), colour, 16 mm, 60 min.
Ritratto di Catherine Spaak (1977), colour, 16 mm, 60 min.

All the above films were made for Italian television, for which she recently directed a series of reportages for the programme *Odeon*.

GABRIELLA ROSALEVA

Una Maria del '23 (1979), colour, Super-8, 25 min.
Trilogia (Cornelia, L'Isola Virginia, La borsetta scarlatta) (1981), colour, Super-8, 60 min.
Processo a Caterina Ross (1982), colour, 16 mm, 60 min.
La vocazione (1983), colour, video, 30 min (made for television).
I luoghi del rito (1983), colour, video, 30 min (made for television).
Egizi: uomini del passato futuro (1983), colour, video, 30 min (made for television).
Cercando Bill (1984), black and white, video, 30 min (made for television).
Viaggio in Senegal (1985), colour, 16 mm, 30 min.
Spartacus (1985), colour, 16 mm, 30 min (one episode in the film *Prima del futuro*).
Sonata a Kreutzer (1985), colour, 16 mm, 100 min (made for television).
Naufragio del galeone Grande San Juan (in production) colour, 35 mm.

SOFIA SCANDURRA

Io sono mia (1977), colour, 35 mm, 90 min.

Since 1978 she has been working for Italian television for which she has made reportages on sociological themes.

The film-maker Gabriella Rosaleva (centre)

CHIARA SCAVIA

L'attesa (1984), colour, 16 mm, 7 min.

VALENTINA SEBASTIANI

Movimento della città (1980), colour, 16 mm, 20 min.
Aldis (1982), black and white, 16 mm, 40 min.
L'incontro (1983), colour, 16 mm, 6 min.

TERESA STANCHI

Quinta generazione (1984), colour, Super-8, 25 min (co-directed with Valerio Vicentini).

MARIA SERENA TAIT

Cinquecento blu notte (1984), colour, video, 24 min.

Since 1978 she has made various reportages for Italian television.

ANNAMARIA TATÒ

Le serpentine d'oro (1978), colour, 35 mm, 37 min.
Apocamonkey (1978), colour, 16 mm, 50 min.
Il doppio sogno dei signori X (1980), colour, 35 mm, 60 min.
Desiderio (1983), colour, 35 mm, 95 min.

She has made various programmes for Italian television including biographies of directors and documentaries on cinema.

ELDA TATTOLI

Appunti (1968), black and white, 5 min.
Il pianeta Venere (1972), colour, 35 mm, 90 min.
Canto d'amore (1985), colour, 35 mm, 90 min.

She has collaborated with Marco Bellocchio on many films, and
co-directed with him *Amore e rabbia*.

CINZIA TORRINI

Prima o poi (1977), colour, 16 mm, 45 min (documentary).
Das Gesicht (1978), colour, 16 mm, 16 min (documentary).
Sanierung in Siena oder die Burocratie ist eine Raupe (1977/81),
    colour, 16 mm, 45 min (documentary).
Ancora una corsa (1981), colour, 16 mm, 67 min.
Giocare d'azzardo (1982), colour, 35 mm, 90 min.
Il ventre di Napoli (1984), colour, 16 mm, 10 min (made for televi-
    sion.
Pozzuoli, la guerra dei poveri (1984), colour, 16 mm, 10 min (made
    for television).
Il mostro di Firenze (1984) (censored).
Somali Women in Action (1985), colour, 16 mm, 30 min.
Hotel Colonial (1987), colour, 35 mm.

ELISABETTA VALGIUSTI

Il nastro di Arianna (1983), colour, video, 60 min.
Finalmente morta (1984), colour, 16 mm, 75 min.

LUCIA VASILICO

Mater admirabilis (1981), colour, Super-8, 100 min.

LINA WERTMULLER

I basilischi (1963), black and white, 35 mm, 84 min.
Questa volta parliamo di uomini (1965), black and white, 35 mm, 91 min.
Gianburrasca (1966), black and white, 35 mm, seven 60-min instalments (made for Italian television).
Mimì metallurgico ferito nell'onore (1972), colour, 35 mm, 121 min.
Film d'amore e d'anarchia ovvero stamattina alle dieci in Via dei Fiori nella nota casa di tolleranza (1973), colour, 35 mm, 125 min.
Tutto a posto e niente in ordine (1974), colour, 35 mm, 110 min.
Travolti da un insolito destino nell'azzurro mare d'agosto (1975), colour, 35 mm, 125 min.
Pasqualino Settebellezze (1975), colour, 35 mm, 123 min.
La fine del mondo nel nostro solito letto in una notte piena di pioggia (1977), colour, 35 mm, 90 min.
Fatto di sangue tra due uomini per causa di una vedova: si sospettano motivi politici (1978), colour, 35 mm, m. 3374.

(left to right) The film-maker Cinzia Torrini with Robert Duvall and John Savage on the set of *Hotel Colonial* (1987), directed by Torrini

Una domenica sera di novembre (1981), colour, 35 mm, 120 min.
Scherzo (1982), colour, 35 mm, 120 min.
Sotto sotto (1983), colour, 35 mm, 120 min.
Complicato intrigo di donne, vicoli e delitti (1985), colour, 35 mm,
    110 min.

References

Albano, Lucilla (ed.) (1987) *Il divano di Freud*, Parma: Pratiche.
Alberti, Giulia (1980) 'La donna, lo sguardo, il desiderio: frattura nel testo classico', *Cinema e Cinema* 25/26
—— (1981) 'Enunciazione e figure femminili nel testo classico', in Giovanna Grignaffini and Piera Detassis (eds) *Sequenza segreta*, Milan: Feltrinelli.
—— (1982) 'Il campo vuoto in *News from Home* : piacere o fascinazione?', in *L'immagine riflessa* (catalogue).
'Alcune femministe milanesi' (1974–5) 'Pratica dell'inconscio e movimento delle donne', *L'erba voglio* 18–19.
Aleramo, Sibilla (1932) *Il passaggio*, Milan: Mondadori.
—— (1942) *Andando e stando*, Milan: Mondadori.
—— (1978) *Diario di una donna*, Milan: Feltrinelli.
—— (1979a) *Un amore insolito*, Milan: Feltrinelli.
—— (1979b) *A woman*, trans. Rosalind Delmar, London: Virago.
—— (1982a) *Amo dunque sono*, Milan: Mondadori.
—— (1982b) *Lettere d'amore a Lina*, Rome: Savelli.
Barthes, Roland (1966) *Critique et vérité*, Paris: Editions du Seuil.
—— (1979) 'Upon leaving the movie theatre', *University Publishing* 6.
—— (1984) *Camera Lucida*, London: Fontana.
Baudry, Jean-Louis (1976) 'The apparatus', *Camera Obscura* 1.
Bazin, André (1972) *What is Cinema?*, Vol. II, Berkeley and Los Angeles: University of California Press.
Bellour, Raymond (1979) 'The unattainable text', *Screen* 16(3).
Benveniste, Emile (1966) *Problèmes de linguistique générale*, Paris: Gallimard.
Bocchetti, Alessandra, 'L'indecente differenza', unpublished.

Brunetta, Gianpiero (1983) 'Il cinema popolare: la visione, la festa e il mito', in *Cinema e storia*, Rimini: Paggioli.

Burch, Noel (1973) *Theory of Film Practice*, London: Secker & Warburg.

Capomazza, Tilde (1981) 'Si dice donna' in *Di fronte allo schermo*, Florence: La Casa Usher.

Cavarero, Adriana, *et al.* (1987) *Diotima. Il pensiero della differenza sessuale*, Milan: La Tartaruga.

Conti, Bruna (ed.) (1978) *La donna e il femminismo. Sibilla Aleramo*, Rome: Editori Riuniti.

Conti, Bruna and Morino, Alba (eds) (1981) *Sibilla Aleramo e il suo tempo*, Milan: Feltrinelli.

de Lauretis, Teresa (1982) *Alice Doesn't: Feminism, Semiotics, Cinema*, Bloomington: Indiana University Press.

Eco, Umberto (1976) *A Theory of Semiotics*, Bloomington: Indiana University Press.

Fachinelli, Elvio (1983) *Claustrofilia*, Milan: Adelphi.

Foucault, Michel (1979) 'What is an author?', *Screen* 20 (1).

Freud, Sigmund (1973) 'The interpretation of dreams', *The Standard Edition*, Vol. V, London: Hogarth Press.

—— (1973) 'A case of hysteria', *The Standard Edition*, Vol. VII, London: Hogarth Press.

—— (1973) 'The ego and the id', *The Standard Edition*, Vol. XIX, London: Hogarth Press.

—— (1973) 'Formulations on the two principles of mental functioning', *The Standard Edition*, Vol. XII, London: Hogarth Press.

—— (1973) 'Group psychology and the analysis of the ego', *The Standard Edition*, Vol. XVIII, London: Hogarth Press.

—— (1964) 'New introductory lectures on psychoanalysis', *The Standard Edition*, Vol. XXII, London: Hogarth Press.

—— (1973) 'An outline of psychoanalysis', *The Standard Edition*, Vol. XXIII, London: Hogarth Press.

Graham, Mark (1981) 'The inaccessibility of *The Lady from Shanghai*', *Film Criticism* V (3).

Grignaffini, Giovanna (1982) 'Verità e poesia: ancora di Silvana e del cinema italiano', *Cinema e Cinema* 30.

Grignaffini, Giovanna and Detassis, Piera (eds) (1981) *Sequenza segreta*, Milan: Feltrinelli.

Irigaray, Luce (1985) *Ethique de la différance sexuelle*, Paris: Les Editions de Minuit.

Kierkegaard, Soren (1940) *Stages on Life's Way*, London: Oxford University Press.

Kristeva, Julia (1983) *Histoires d'amour*, Paris: Denoel.

Laplanche, Jean, and Pontalis, Jean-Baptiste, (1973) *The Language of Psychoanalysis*, London: Hogarth Press and Institute of Psychoanalysis.

Libreria delle donne di Milano (1987) *Non credere di avere dei diritti*, Turin: Rosenberg & Sellier.

Mantegazza, Paolo (1879) *Fisiologia dell'amore*, Milan: Gaetano Britano e Comp.

Maraini, Dacia (1979) 'Tema', *Lessico politico delle donne* 6.

Matte Blanco, Ignacio, (1975) *The Unconscious as Infinite Sets*, London: Duckworth

Melandri, Lea (1977) *L'infamia originaria*, Milan: L'Erba Voglio.

—— (forthcoming) *L'estasi e il gelo*, Milan: Rizzoli.

Melchiori, Paola (ed.) (1987) *Verifica d'identità. Materiali, esperienze, riflessioni sul fare cultura tra donne*, Rome: Utopia.

Melchiori, Paola and Scattigno, Anna (1986) *Simone Weil*, Milan: La Salamandra.

Metz, Christian (1977) *Le signifiant imaginaire*, Paris: Union Générale d'Editions.

Miscuglio, Annabella, and Daopoulo, Rony, (eds) (1980) *Kinomato. La donna nel cinema*, Bari: Dedalo Libri.

Mitry, Jean (1965) *Esthétique et psychologie du cinéma*, Paris: Editions Universitaires.

Mulvey, Laura (1975) 'Visual pleasure and narrative cinema', *Screen* Autumn.

Musil, Robert (1979) *The Man without Qualities*, London: Picador/Pan.

Orlando, Francesco (1982) *Illuminismo e retorica freudiana*, Turin: Einaudi.

Paliotti, Vittorio and Grano, Enzo (1969) *Napoli nel cinema*, Naples.

Piccone, Stella Simonetta (1980) 'Crescere negli anni '50', *Memoria* 7/8.

Quaglietti, Lorenzo (1980) *Storia economico-politica del cinema italiano 1945–1960*, Rome: Editori Riuniti.

Scheler, Max (1979) *Pudore e sentimento del pudore*, Naples: Guida Editori.

Schnitzler, Arthur. (1929) *Teresa* (preface by S. Aleramo), Milan: Soc. Anon. 'Modernissima'.

Sontag, Susan (1977) *On Photography*, New York: Farrar, Straus & Giroux.

Sorlin, Pierre (1977) *Sociologie du cinéma*, Paris: Aubier Montaigne.

Tsvetaeva, Marina (1982) *Il racconto di Sonecka*, Milan: Editori Riuniti.

Violi, Patrizia (1986) *L'infinito singolare*, Verona: Essedue Edizioni.

Weiniger, Otto (1906) *Sex and Character*, London: Heinemann.

Wittels, Fritz (1962) *Minutes of the Vienna Psychoanalytic Society*, Vol. I, New York: International Universities Press.

Woolf, Virginia (1929) *A Room of One's Own*, London: Hogarth Press.

—— (1971) *Night and Day*, London: Hogarth Press.

Index